Made To Care

Ann Bird

Published by
Methodist Publishing House

ISBN 1 85852 028 2

Published by
Methodist Publishing House
20 Ivatt Way, Peterborough PE3 7PG

Printed by
Clifford Frost Limited, Lyon Road,
Windsor Avenue, London SW19 2SE.

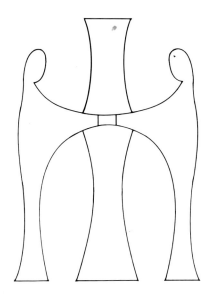

CONTENTS

Page

Acknowledgements   2

Preface   3

The Fruits of the Spirit *Love, Joy, Peace, Patience, Kindness, Goodness, Faithfulness, Gentleness, Self Control*   5

Gracious Moments   24

Care-less words? *Saying 'No', Laughter, Failure, Anger*   39

Elements of Caring *Earth, Air, Fire, Water*   48

Meditations for Advent and Christmas   60

Words of Freedom *Acceptance, Forgiveness, Affirmation*   74

Epilogue   95

Copyright acknowledgements   98

ACKNOWLEDGEMENTS

The articles in this book were all originally written for publication in the *Methodist Recorder* and I am deeply grateful to the Editor, Michael Taylor, for his unfailing encouragement and support both in this project and in many other ways over the past seven years. It is with his kind permission that the articles are reproduced in this form.

New material includes a few of my own poems as well as extracts which seem to have particular significance in relation to the rest of the material.

To be able to include the coloured pictures of the banners gives me special pleasure. During my time as Pastoral Care Secretary, Win Field has created several banners for me with loving and imaginative skill. They have been an inspiration to me, and, I believe, to all who have seen them as their symbolism and colour have drawn us deeper into an understanding of our pastoral ministry together. To Win, and to Mary and Grace, her willing helpers, I acknowledge an immense debt of gratitude.

And finally I want to say thank you to Brian Thornton and to Edith Coole and to the rest of the staff at Methodist Publishing House. In particular, Brian and Edith's support and patience and willingness to help has been a tremendous source of strength. As we have produced various resources together over the years I have not only valued their expertise and standards of excellence, I have also been enriched by their friendship and grateful for their pastoral care of me personally.

Ann Bird

PREFACE

We love because He first loved us. (1 John 4:19)

Christian caring grows out of our understanding of the nature of God and our experience of receiving his love and care in our own lives. We were indeed 'made to care', created to be in relationship with God and with one another and to do all in our power to contribute to the wholeness of life in all its aspects. However, like all other Gospel imperatives, this one, too, presents us with an invitation to challenge and risk as well as with a sense of belonging and a promise of acceptance.

God's care is for *all* people and if we try in any measure to reflect his love, we cannot ever be content with a cosy pastoral intention which reaches out only to those who respond lovingly to us or who contribute to our own need for comfort and security. The more we become aware of God's love for us and for his creation the more we find ourselves being 'made' or compelled to care in a bewildering variety of ways.

Of course the obvious arena for our ministry of caring is in the day-to-day routine of our lives, and we will want always to be aware of ways in which we can understand and respond to what others feel and experience as we spend time with them at work or in leisure. Pastoral caring can never be isolated from the mission of the church or from our social responsibility and, if loving in Christ's name means entering deeply into people's pain and hurt, it will inevitably involve us eventually in a struggle against injustice, greed, power-seeking or violence. We are to care for the despairing and the rejected; for the poor and marginalised; for those who are alone; and for the broken in heart and spirit.

When I first became Pastoral Care Secretary for the Methodist Division of Ministries I tried to spell out my vision for my future ministry in a *Methodist Recorder* article. The two quotations that I used then remain as central to my vision now as they were all that time ago and they are worth drawing out from that first article and sharing with you again. The first is from Angela Tilby who, in *Won't You Join The Dance*, says –

3

To be persons, in the Christian sense, means that we must bear one another's burdens. We must be prepared to suffer pain for one another and to carry each other in love through times of darkness and dread. We must take on what we can of each other's violence and woundedness without allowing ourselves the relief of retaliation. Only if we are prepared to do this do we enter the privilege of the Gospel, which is to heal each other and find our healing in and through each other.

To have the ability to 'carry each other in love' is a gift of the Spirit which can, in a sense, neither be taught nor controlled. Yet it is a gift freely given when we are prepared to become vulnerable, responsive human beings, alive to the unique potential of each person and to the possibility of grace and forgiveness in every situation. We can make it all seem so complicated, yet in God's reality caring is so very natural, as my second quotation makes abundantly clear.

A Greek Orthodox nun working in India with leprosy patients was asked by a visiting bishop if she had 'learned the language of the natives'. She hesitated for a moment and then replied –

Oh, yes, your Grace, I learned five of them –
The language of smiling,
The language of weeping,
The language of touching,
The language of listening,
And the language of loving.

I still believe these are languages we can learn together and that they can enable us to become the loving friends to each other we were created to be. To be 'made to care' is a high privilege and a lifetime's ministry. The articles that follow attempt in some small way to encourage and affirm us in ways that make such caring possible.

Ann Bird

THE FRUITS OF THE SPIRIT
AND PASTORAL CARE

The fruit of the spirit is love, joy, peace, patience, kindness, goodness, faithfulness, gentleness, self control.
(Gal. 5:22)

Love

Spirit of love within me,
Possess my hands and heart;
Break through the bonds of self-concern
That seeks to stand apart;
Grant me the love that suffers long,
That hopes, believes and bears,
The love fulfilled in sacrifice
That cares as Jesus cares.

Timothy Dudley-Smith

Christian love and caring is essentially a response to God's love for us. 'We love because he first loved us' and thus our care for others grows out of our understanding of God's love and care in our own lives. So, too, the pastoral care which should be at the heart of the Church's life and ministry is a response of gratitude to the love and care of God for us in Christ.

When Jesus met with people in Galilee and Capernaum he loved them in such a way that he obviously felt with them in the centre of his being, and that is our calling too – to become deeply sensitive to others in our own family and neighbourhood, in our own 'Galilee' areas, so that the way in which we love is a sign of the presence of God in our lives as clearly as it was a sign of God's presence in the life of Jesus.

But how much easier it is to say or write such words than it is to act upon them! All too conscious of our own inadequacies, our tiredness, our inability to make friends or even to like certain people, we often feel that we are defeated before we begin our pastoral ministry and that anyway we are too much in need of love and understanding ourselves to have sufficient strength to offer such self-emptying love to others. Moreover we forget, that we are not asked to share our strength so much as our vulnerability and that God is not setting us impossible goals but inviting us to open ourselves in friendship and concern to each other. What we have in common together is our humanity and we are all capable of being truly present to each other if we remember that God is always truly present with us as well.

Mother Teresa speaks of love as 'a fruit that is in season at all times, and within reach of every hand. Anyone may gather it and no limit is set.' If this is so – and it is a belief at the heart of the Christian Gospel – of what variety is this fruit of love that can be so easily harvested in the field of pastoral care?

It is a fruit that grows out of the soil of loving ourselves positively enough to be of service to others, and it is rooted in our ability to grow towards wholeness in our own experience of hurt and pain. It is ripe with the possibility of expanding our own world and that of other people – so that as we give and receive love one with another we encourage each other to grow and to be healed. At its core, its centre, is the desire to affirm others, to sustain them and to accept them, and to offer friendship which is both practical and reliable, both committed and selfless.

Love of this kind is not dependent simply on feelings. It wants the best for anyone with whom we come into contact and is glad to give others their freedom as God gives us our freedom. Such love can be very painful and time-consuming. Such love can demand political involvement and social awareness. Such love can bring joy and fulfilment and a deeper awareness of the suffering love of God and of humanity.

We cannot know when we set out on the path of love where it will lead us. What we can be sure of is that without such love no other fruit of the spirit can really thrive and that the more we seek a loving relationship with our neighbours the more we will find we are in a loving relationship with God.

Joy

O God, the source of the whole world's
gladness and bearer of its pain.
May your unconquerable joy rest at the
heart of all our trouble and distress. Amen

This would not have been a prayer on the lips of Jews living in
Old Testament times for to them joy was, above all, a sign of
prosperity and material blessing. Joy and pain were mutually
exclusive and the contrast between them is epitomised in the
words of the Psalmist: 'Weeping may endure for a night, but joy
cometh in the morning.'

But in the New Testament writings it is different. There
are numerous references to joy as something which arises out of
suffering and which is to be welcomed rather than shunned. The
inter-mingling of pain and joy is not only evident but also to be
embraced.

'My dear friends, do not be bewildered by the fiery ordeal
that is upon you as though it were something extraordinary. It
gives you a share in Christ's sufferings and that is cause for joy.'
(1 Peter 4:12, 13.)

And again: 'My brothers, count it all joy when you have
to face trials of many kinds.' (James 1:2.)

Suffering as 'cause for joy' has been echoed in Christian
hymns.

I thank thee more that all our joy
    Is touched with pain.
That shadows fall on brightest hours,
    That thorns remain,
So that earth's bliss may be our guide,
    And not our chain.

– but I am uneasy about that particular emphasis. I wonder how
many of us can really sing those lines in total honesty? I know

7

that life is so ordered that change and suffering are inevitable – that I can accept – but when I love my family or friends it is not my natural reaction to thank God because my relationship with them is broken by death, not do I thank God if I am the one to contract an incurable disease. On the other hand – and this I find far more satisfying theologically – not only do I thank God with a full heart for moments of pure joy but I also discover that if I have the courage and grace to work through suffering and grief there can in the end be a very special kind of joy at the very heart of that pain and that suffering.

I imagine this is the kind of joy that the blind George Mathieson, who had just been jilted by his fiancée, experienced –

O Joy that seekest me through pain
I cannot close my heart to thee;
I trace the rainbow through the rain
And feel the promise is not vain
That morn shall tearless be.

The words in the original version, so we learn from the *Companion to Hymns & Psalms*, were even more triumphant. 'I climb the rainbow through the rain' and that seems a far more combative, right way of approaching suffering than merely thanking God for it. We have all visited people who have made us feel very humble when we go intending to offer love and care only to discover that, because they have 'climbed the rainbow' through their own pain and hurt, they radiate a joy and serenity which ministers to us and brings us joy.

John Powell, in his book *Happiness is an Inside Job*, tells of a man he knew named Frank who was liked by everyone. He was warm and kind and always appreciative of people. Then Frank died suddenly. He left scarcely anything in worldly terms but he had left something very precious, two pages of writing entitled 'A List of my Special Pleasures'. According to this list Frank had enjoyed many things during his lifetime – scenic trails, writing congratulatory notes, picture albums, the Boston Pops Orchestra . . . and the last four entries in his list were all the same – ice-cream, ice-cream, ice-cream, ice-cream. Frank had had many private sufferings but somehow he always managed to enjoy day-to-day living and that showed in his treatment of other people.

It is strange how often we need to be reminded that pastoral care is not just about standing alongside those who need our support in time of difficulty but that it is just as important to recognise and celebrate other people's joyful moments in life, their successes, their happiness. Caring is about sending a note of congratulation as Frank did; about being glad for someone who has had a promotion or whose daughter has achieved a university entrance. It's about throwing a party and about loving people enough really to want the best for them. We are often far better at 'weeping with those who weep' than 'rejoicing with those who rejoice'. In fact, to our shame, we tend to feel jealous of the joyful and we try to play down their achievements or to injure their sense of well-being ever so slightly. But if we really care for people we shall be glad for them and with them.

Other people may not agree with me but I tend to see happiness in terms of laughter and movement and as something good in itself but fairly ephemeral. Joy, on the other hand, is something much deeper, longer lasting, more 'silent'. And I think that that is reflected in the way joy arises in our caring ministry. I heard recently of a woman called Lucy who lived in an old people's home. She was more fit than many in the home and so she decided to grow flowers so that she could cut them, take them to her more confined friends and spend time with them when she visited. A lovely way to bring joy to others – and such joy-bearing occasions are possible for all of us if we set our hearts and wills on discovering this 'unconquerable joy' in our own lives whatever our circumstances.

Peace

Let peace stream out before you. Let
peace stream to the left of you. Let
peace stream to the right of you. Let
peace remain awhile wherever you may
tread. May it spread even to the
furthest boundaries of the universe –
peace.

Julia de Beausobre was undergoing torture and interrogation in a Russian prison when she became aware of what she described as 'an inaudible voice of tragic beauty' enveloping her with those words. When I read them, while recognising their unique and visionary quality, I was reminded of our youngest son, during his training at drama school, speaking of the way in which the students were taught to be aware of the kind of 'space' they created around themselves, the kind of space they left behind them.

In the context of the stage the drama students were learning to be aware of the effect of the intensity of their emotions and the authenticity of their character portrayal, but I found this a fascinating thought because I believe we can all learn to be conscious of something similar happening in our day-to-day lives. I began to wonder what kind of space people perceive around me and what kind of atmosphere I engender in my relationship with people. Not, I am sure, the kind of peaceful, serene atmosphere I would dearly like it to be, and I imagine I am not alone in that!

And yet, how important it is in relating to others to be peaceful people. They are the people to whom we turn most naturally in times of crisis. They are the people who have learnt to come to terms with their own experience in such a way that they have achieved a serenity which can at times be almost tangible. They are the people . . . but, wait a moment, how easy it is to distance God's truth! *We* are the people to whom Jesus said 'Peace is my parting gift to you, my own peace, such as the world cannot give . . .' *We* are the people who were enjoined to 'be at peace with one another because we follow the Prince of Peace who came to guide our feet into the way of peace'.

It should be natural for all Christians to be peace-full people, not because life is any easier for us than for others or because we are naturally placid by temperament but because we should be so rooted and grounded in the peace of Christ that this peace becomes part of our own nature. We should leave peace in the space behind us as we walk through life and peace should 'remain wherever we may tread'. Peace, in fact, is one of the greatest gifts we have to offer in our caring ministry and it is something, as well, which most people are seeking.

We want peace for each other, we want peace for ourselves, we want people to be at peace with God and with each other, we want peace in our communities, in our families and in the wider world. We want the kind of peace for everyone that our Jewish friends speak of as Shalom.

But peace does not come easily as we all know. It has to be worked at and prayed for and it involves single-mindedness and acceptance of situations or relationships or limitations which we find frustrating or painful. It is not a weak quality but one born out of perseverance and prayer, humility and self-lessness. Yet those who have peace to offer others – those who are peace-full people – are a real blessing in the world and to be a peace-maker is a pastoral ministry in which we are all involved. We are called to 'go in peace in the power of the Spirit' as we exercise a ministry of reconciliation with understanding and love.

Show us, good Lord, the peace we should seek,
the peace we must give,
the peace we must keep,
the peace we must forgo
and the peace you have given us in Jesus our Lord.
Amen.

Patience

The Beatitudes of the Mentally Handicapped

Blessed are you who take time to listen to difficult speech, for you help us to know that if we persevere we can be understood.

Blessed are you who walk with us in public places, and ignore the stares of strangers, for in your companionship we find havens of relaxation.

Blessed are you who never bid us to 'hurry up', and more blessed are you who do not snatch our tasks from our hands to do them for us, for often we need time rather than help.

Blessed are you who stand beside us as we enter new and untried ventures, for our failures will be outweighed by the times we surprise ourselves and you.

Blessed are you who ask for our help, for our greatest need is to be needed.

Blessed are you when by all ways you assure us that the things that make us individuals are not our peculiar muscles, nor our wounded nervous systems, nor our difficulties in learning, but are in the God-given self which no infirmities can confine.

Rejoice and be exceedingly glad, and know that you give us reassurance that could never be spoken in words, for you deal with us as Christ dealt with his children.

Anon

Kindness

Be kind and merciful. Let no one ever come to you without coming away better and happier. Be the living expression of God's kindness: kindness in your face, kindness in your smile, kindness in your warm greeting. In the slums we are the light of God's kindness to the poor. To children, to the poor, to all who suffer and are lonely, give always a happy smile –

Give them not only your care, but also your heart.

Mother Teresa of Calcutta

Kindness, loving kindness, motivated by my love, is a mark of my grace in you. Be kind to one another and let others show kindness to you.

I am kind to you all without favour or reserve. My wonderful kindness to you is like the blue of a fair day, like the soft rain in the growing season. It is the touch of one who loves you, the smile of one who cares for you.

In my kindness there is nothing violent, nothing abrasive, but I give out my kindness with openhanded gentleness.

Kindness is at first in your hearts, then in your words and deeds. Be kind to one another. Be open to give and receive kindness.

Judith Pinhey

Goodness

When I watched the 'Barchester Towers' television series I was reminded of the way in which Anthony Trollope speaks of Mr Harding at the end of the novel.

'The author now leaves him in the hands of his readers; not as a hero, not as the man to be admired and talked of, not as a man who should be toasted at public dinners and spoken of with conventional absurdity as a perfect divine, but as a good man without guile, believing humbly in the religion which he has striven to teach and guided by the precepts which he has striven to learn.'

Of all the characters at Barchester, Septimus Harding appeared to be the most whole, the most mature, the most 'good', and yet he himself was always conscious of his own failings and what he saw as his lack of charity. Such humility is, however, surely one of the chief marks of a truly good person; not the spurious humility for which Uriah Heep is infamous but the humility that measures itself against the goodness of God. For, if we so order our lives that we keep always before us such a vision of God, then other events and people and priorities will fall into proper perspective and we shall be less preoccupied with our own concerns and more conscious of other people's needs and claims upon us.

But we would be mistaken if we saw such goodness in too passive a light. The vision of God's goodness will not just affect ourselves. It will frequently impel us to work for change or to see right and wrong more clearly. It will save us from being too narrow in our thinking or our loving and will encourage us to see others with greater understanding and compassion. It will help us, too, not to take ourselves too seriously!

Clifford Longley writes of the way in which good people 'can sometimes be slightly daft; though many of them do manage to have their heads screwed on exceedingly tight. And unlike ordinary people trying to be pious, they can also be fun to be with.' On the other hand, we must bear in mind that a proper self-love is actually part of true humility because when we love ourselves we are loving that which God loves.

There is, though, no short cut to goodness. 'Teach us how to grow in goodness' we sang as children and we have to be prepared to change and mature through a lifetime if we are to attain at all to the goodness for which we long, the goodness that loves people not because of their attractiveness, abilities or achievement, or even the lack of them, but because they are themselves, unique beings loved by God.

And if we think in terms of our pastoral ministry – how does goodness manifest itself? I think it has much to do with our being genuine, warm and accepting of others. As we centre ourselves more completely in the goodness of God and become more whole and integrated people, the better we are able truly to see and to love and to help our neighbours. Moreover, in society as a whole, the goodness of the Church will have something to do with coming to grips with all that militates against human beings growing towards their full humanity and with creating a world where goodness is a transforming reality rather than an unattainable goal.

Mr Harding, for all his gentleness and selflessness in relationships, was concerned with social goodness as well as with his own dependence upon God. So, in our journey towards goodness, even though our thoughts and wills are directed heavenwards, we need to keep our feet firmly on the ground of our experience if we are to allow the fruit of 'goodness' to mature in a way that is most likely to bring wholeness to ourselves and to others.

Holy Spirit, dwell with me;
I myself would holy be;
Separate from sin, I would
Choose and cherish all things good.

Thomas Tokelynch

Faithfulness

Faithful God,
by faith
may we conquer
our deepest fears.
By faithful action
may the chains of poverty be broken.
By faithful struggle
may the web of oppression be
overcome.
By faithful commitment
may the walls that divide fall.

Kate McMilhagga

Our Lord and reason do not demand results in the things we do,
but only our faithful and whole-hearted co-operation, endeavour
and diligence, for these do depend on us, whereas success does
not.

St Francis de Sales

It's very hard, Lord
to love the unlovely.

I know your commandments
off by heart
but that is only a beginning.
Your Kingdom is beyond
the recitation of the familiar.

Write your law of love
not upon my memory only
but upon my heart
so that it is strained
and tested daily
as I am faced by
the loneliness of my friends next door
the desperation of my friends across the world.

May my prayers be said
and my tears be shed
for the countless thousands
who are denied the presence
of human love
and who therefore believe
they are out of range of yours.

May my prejudices be stripped
and my ignorance challenged
as I come to terms
with the new neighbours you show me
on my pilgrimage.

And when people
try to persuade me to give up
may I still insist
on travelling the extra mile
that love demands.

David Jenkins

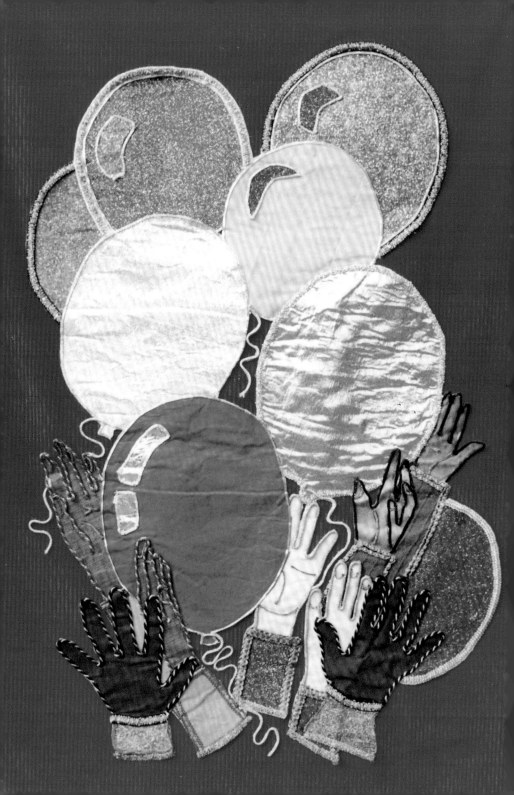

Gentleness

Bound together in life we care for each other as fragile human beings, free to be ourselves, yet vulnerable and needing to be a recognised part of the whole pattern and dance of life.

Our circumstances change in the same way that the position of the balloons is changed by the wind. At times life feels good. We shall be at the centre of things, happy to be alive, vibrant – at times we shall want to hide away from life, we shall be damaged by our experiences.

Rejoicing in our differences of race and culture we shall endeavour to hold each other gently, offering each other up to God as if with the gentleness of gloved hands.

We shall be aware of the breath of God around and within us.

* * * * *

To give life
is to be full of sacred wonder and reverence
in front of the mystery of the person;
it is to see the beauty
within and beyond all that is broken.

To love is not to give of your riches
but to reveal to others their riches, their gifts, their value,
and to trust them and their capacity to grow.

So it is important to approach people
in their brokenness and littleness
gently,
so gently,
not forcing yourself upon them,
but accepting them as they are,
with humility and respect.

Jean Vanier

Self Control

On their 50th wedding anniversary a couple were asked to sum up the reasons for their long and happy marriage.

The husband said: 'I have tried never to be selfish. After all, there is no "I" in the word "marriage".'

The wife added: 'For my part, I have tried never to correct my husband's spelling!'

That is the kind of loving self-control which escapes most of us – but it is a light-hearted example of one way in which we can exercise restraint in our relationships with others and it has something to do with recognising priorities.

We can be so quick to point out people's inadequacies and short-comings or to correct their mistakes that we fail to offer them the kindness and gentleness that we are always wanting for ourselves. Of course there are occasions when we need to 'speak the truth in love' to each other. The trouble is we so often forget the importance of 'love' in that phrase and seem almost to take pleasure in discomfiting others. It is surely better to 'keep the "I" out of marriage' rather than to insist on its being there with the possibility of diminishing both the other person and the relationship between us.

Self control needs to be exercised in our caring ministry in varied ways. We are so apt to talk about our own concerns ad infinitum rather than giving others space and time to share *their* needs and concerns with us. And when we *have* listened and have perhaps heard something of which we do not in our heart of hearts approve, how quickly we can become judgmental or critical rather than accepting and understanding.

On the other hand we can sometimes be too 'understanding'. For instance, it is not helpful to say to someone who has just been bereaved – 'I know exactly how you feel. I remember when my husband died I felt exactly as you do.' No-one knows exactly how someone else feels. No-one experiences bereavement in exactly the same way as anyone else. In any case, no-one who has just been bereaved can cope with someone else's bereavement story, however well-intentioned the offering of shared experience may be. In circumstances of grief, as in so many others, what is needed from us as carers is simply to be with the bereaved person, listening to them in such a way that they are assured of our desire to stay alongside them, accepting their reaction to what has happened for as long as is necessary.

Self control in pastoral care is, however, not only about putting the other person's needs first or even about spending a lifetime trying, with God's help, to control our temper and selfishness, our need for recognition or our desire for the limelight in one way or another. It is also about disciplining ourselves to spend time with God in such a way that we gradually become relaxed, loving, Christ-like people who give and receive care naturally and in whose lives the fruits of the Spirit are self-evident.

In the January 1988 edition of *Christian* Angela Ashwin wrote: 'It is both hilarious and inevitable that our sublimest longings for God are mixed up with day-dreams about holidays and pet hamsters and the bank balance. Far more dangerous are distractions about the spiritual progress we are making: "I'm doing rather well," we think to ourselves. "My distractions are getting less and less." This is the biggest distraction of them all. It can be quite a struggle to let go of this particular balloon into the wind of God's Spirit, in order to free ourselves again to ask "What do I really seek? Splendid thoughts about God and my prayer – or God himself."'

That is the right way round, not just about our prayer life but about our pastoral ministry. If we try to acquire each of the fruits of the Spirit individually and in our own strength we shall undoubtedly fail. But if we rest in the love of God as our first priority others will increasingly find God's love, patience, kindness . . . in us. That is all they need from us.

Holy Spirit,
in our homes and community
but especially in the household of faith,

may we walk in love.

Holy Spirit,
when we worship and witness
and when we share the sufferings of our neighbours,

may we walk in joy.

Holy Spirit,
in places of confrontation,
racial unrest, stark inequality and deep-seated violence,

may we walk in peace.

Holy Spirit,
in a frantic and fearful world
where there are pressures to gain quick results,

may we walk in patience.

Holy Spirit,
as we seek to respect other people's personalities,
their gifts and skills, their jobs and dreams,

may we walk in kindness.

Holy Spirit,
in our determination to reject what is unjust,
hypocritical and an affront to the Gospel,

may we walk in goodness.

Holy Spirit,
where we have made commitments to those close to us
and promises to love you and our neighbours,

may we walk in faithfulness.

Holy Spirit,
when we are tempted to respond with anger
to embittering situations which are already filled with pain,

may we walk in gentleness.

Holy Spirit,
in our private living and public responsibilities
and in all our decision-making,
may we walk with self control.

Holy Spirit,
fill us and all people with these gifts now and always.

David Jenkins

You can never trust God too much.
Why is it that some people do not bear fruit?
It is because they have no trust
either in God or in themselves.

Meister Eckhart

GRACIOUS MOMENTS

I love Elizabeth Jennings' poetry. She speaks of experiences I recognise and shares insights into feelings of pain and joy that belong to us all. One poem is particularly precious:

I count the moments of my mercies up,
I make a list of love and find it full.
I do all this before I fall asleep.

Others examine consciences. I tell
My beads of gracious moments shining still . . .

St Paul would surely have approved of such an ending to the day – 'Whatsoever things are pure . . . lovely . . . of good report . . . think on these things' (Phil:4).

What frequently surprises me, though, is that it is not always the large, important happening that warms me most, becomes a 'shining bead' for me, but the thoughtful comment, the tentative touch of a hand, the note dropped through the door, the conversation on the telephone.

How often do we miss chances to care for people in these relatively simple ways because we are afraid of being misunderstood, or of being sentimental or of getting the moment wrong? Yet I believe if we are really listening to other people, really trying to understand what matters to them at any particular moment we can easily see opportunities to demonstrate our oneness with them in ways that show we care.

We take it for granted that we will write a letter expressing sympathy to someone who has been bereaved, or a note of appreciation to the preacher for a particularly helpful sermon. But it is so important on other occasions as well to show people that we have noticed they are finding life difficult, in the hope that it might help them to know that we are thinking about them and praying for them.

A simple note may be all that's needed: 'Dear Brian, You must have found it very hard to cope with your first family service last Sunday so soon after Jane's death. We want you to know that we were thinking about you and will continue to do so. And if at anytime you feel the need for some company, don't hesitate to come round – the coffee pot is always on in this house!'

I still have a little card dropped through our door the day on which my husband 'left home' for six months to work in a refugee camp – 'Dear Ann, May the grace of courage, gaiety and the quiet mind, and all such blessings as come from the Father to his children be yours now and always, Love . . .' Needless to say, that note has found its way permanently on to my 'list of love'.

But it is not only in words that we can care for people in small but sensitive ways. If we cannot visit, we can ring a friend up on the morning of the day she is due to go into hospital; we can phone to hear the results of an interview (and be supportive and affirming if no offer of a job has been forthcoming); we can get in touch with someone whom we know is becoming very tired as a 'carer' and encourage them with our friendship and understanding. For an elderly person living on their own there is great comfort and security in the knowledge that someone will phone them each day just to make sure all is well with them.

The trouble is that we are all so busy that, however good our intentions, we don't always get around to writing that note or making that phone call. That's why, when the letter does drop through the door or the phone does ring, we know that someone really cares enough about us to make time for us.

More rarely, perhaps, for most of us, we can portray our feelings through touch – so difficult for us British! In the final paragraph of John V Taylor's *The Go-Between God* there is a marvellous passage in which he describes the healing touch of one woman's arm around the shoulders of another. Gestures of this kind can mean so much, bridging the gaps between people, giving comfort, sharing pain and expressing love. For example, the way in which we take someone's hands as we give the peace can convey a world of caring. Yet how thoughtless we often are. Are those of us who live in families aware of how seldom some people living on their own are ever touched or ever kissed? Do we ever touch the unlovely, the uncared-for whom we meet?

Elizabeth Jennings goes on to hope that through her own 'gracious moments' she may be healed enough to reach out towards others – in her case through her poetry, in our case by whatever means are most natural to us.

> . . . may they heal
> The pain of silence for all those who stare
> At stars as I do but are helpless to
> Make the bright necklace . . .

We all need to be cared about; we all need these little touches of concern and understanding, so, as we remember the 'mercies' that have meant much to us, let's try also to find time to make sure that others, too, have a 'list of love' to remember at the end of the day.

* * * * *

The impulse of love that leads us to the doorway of a friend is the voice of God within and we need not be afraid to follow it.

Agnes Sanford

CIRCLES OF LOVE

In her book *Sharing the Darkness* Sheila Cassidy writes: 'More than anything I have discovered that the world is not divided into the sick and those who care for them, but that we are all wounded and that we all contain within our hearts that love which is for the healing of the nations. What we lack is the courage to start giving it away.'

Few of us would argue with her perception but I would want to add that many of us also lack the courage to allow ourselves to become vulnerable enough to start 'receiving' love. We find it difficult to do more than pay lip-service to the concept of mutuality of caring. Consequently many people, particularly those, both lay and ordained, who are in leadership positions in the Church, feel inhibited about sharing their concerns or their own 'darkness' in any way that might make them seem dependent on others.

Yet Christian caring is not only about one person helping another, it is also a way of changing the whole fellowship, bringing wholeness and fullness of life and a sense of belonging. And this wholeness is itself creative as it enables those within the loving community to find expression through mutuality – a circular movement of giving and receiving as we become more rounded personalities encircled by each other's concern.

The image of the circle has become very important for me in this context. I have a banner which I use in pastoral care workshops where an open-ended circle appears to enfold the empty cross as symbol of the Church. It is open because it is not exclusive and it reminds us that although our church circles and family circles are vital to us they must never be too inward looking. It frequently happens that in our isolation we are so thankful to be accepted in a particular circle ourselves that we hesitate to turn outwards or to leave a space ready for others to 'join hands' with us and share a sense of companionship.

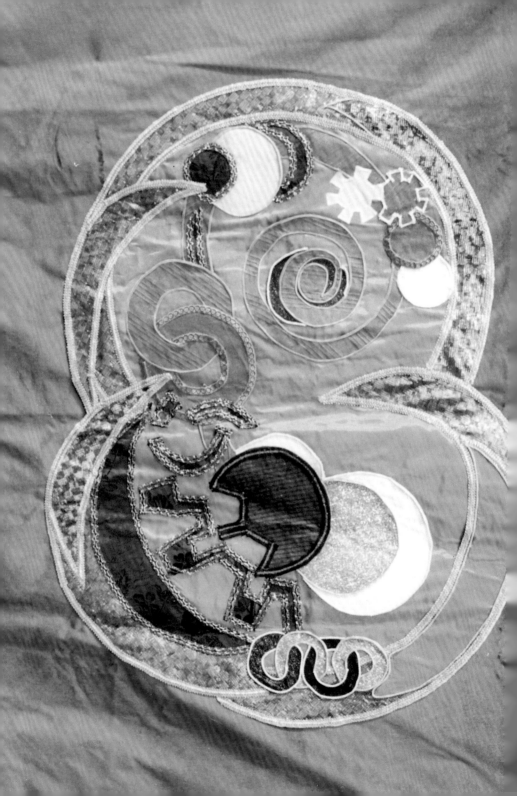

And yet we need to feel safe within our circles, whether it be the house group, the minister's fellowship or a group of personal friends. We need to be able to trust that we are accepted so that we can go beyond the superficialities and allow ourselves to be enfolded and enriched by others' care for us – not easy, but essential if we are to cease trying to 'go it alone' as we so often do.

Of course, circles can be destructive as well. We speak of 'vicious' circles and talk of 'going round in circles'. How often do those of us who find ourselves in positions of leadership feel like that! The pressures can be so intense, the expectation of us so overwhelming that it seems impossible to centre down into ourselves and find direction and purpose.

It makes me think of another kind of circle – that of a 'wheel'. I would have to admit that there moments when I could well liken myself to the wheel of a car! – the pressure at some times is tremendous and I am very aware that there is always the possibility of a slow puncture caused by a number of comparatively small things going wrong until I lose all my energy and drive. Worse still, the sudden puncture, the burst tyre, the unexpected and unnerving experience which stops me in my tracks and makes it difficult for me to get going again without expert repair work and help. Sometimes, too, I lose touch with the energy which makes possible any movement at all – to get 'stuck in a rut' can be as incapacitating as a major breakdown.

To alter the image slightly, a potentially paralysing situation arises when one feels that one is helplessly caught up by 'wheels within wheels' and many of us must sometimes feel that our church structures function in such a complicated way that we are made powerless or become bitter and frustrated.

All these experiences need to be acknowledged and recognised as common to most of us, but personally I know that it is when I am most under pressure that I am least likely to ask for help.

Yet circles are, above all, symbols of hope. Think of the ring given in marriage, the Celtic circle which was said to accompany a person or keep him from dangers and which is so beautifully expressed by David Adam in *The Edge of Glory:*

> Circle me O God
> Keep hope within
> Despair without.
>
> Circle me O God
> Keep peace within
> Keep turmoil out.
>
> Circle me O God
> Keep calm within
> Keep storms without.
>
> Circle me O God
> Keep strength within
> Keep weakness out.

In *Making Sense of Religion* Donald Reeves talks about 'Sarah's circle'. The 'Sarah's circle' of feminist theology, he tells us, is set against the kind of hierarchical 'Jacob's ladder' image which pervades so many of our church and society structures – 'Sarah's circle offers something quite different. It says that God can shatter all known certainties and break through death, hopelessness and barrenness' to offer a promise of a more human and humane future – 'Sarah's circle is one of laughter and joy' and 'in the circle all dance together, supporting and encouraging one another.' What a lovely, joyous image of caring pastoral ministry that becomes.

The universal, timeless dimension of the circle image is implicit in Sarah's circle as it was in Henry Vaughan's vision –

> 'I saw Eternity the other night,
> Like a great ring of pure and endless light,
> All calm, as it was bright.'

It has been said, too, that the nature of God is a circle of which the 'centre is everywhere and the circumference is nowhere,' and Robert Herrick spoke of love as –

A circle that doth restless move
In the same sweet eternity of love.

If God can be imagined in such a way perhaps we would do well to centre our thinking about caring for each other in terms of trying to encompass and encircle one another rather than supporting in hierarchical fashion. And as we encompass each other in love and understanding and interdependence, we shall learn to move forward out of the circles that bind and constrain us and we shall accompany each other into wider spheres with greater compassion and a stronger belief in the love that encircles and surrounds us all.

A Way of Intercession

I brought your tiredness home with me today and
held it in my arms awhile, touching it gently with my
love and hoping to embrace both it and you until
imagination blended into fact – and I was tired **for** you.

I brought your sadness home with me today and
circled it with tender strength, trying with loving
care to bind your soul with mine until you knew
yourself at peace – while I was sad **for** you.

Now that we meet again, I cherish still these gifts of
yours you had not given, and ask if I may keep
them close, drawing them deep into my love so that
my heart can share your pain – and I can ache **for** you.

Ann Bird

The light of God surrounds you,
The love of God enfolds you,
The power of God protects you,
The presence of God watches over you,
Wherever you are, God is.

Source unknown

CANDLES IN THE BREATH OF GOD

The following reflections were prompted in part by an article in *The Independent* entitled 'The back-door approach to dying'.

The central concern expressed was that in many homes for the elderly, staff hide deaths from residents, robbing them of a chance to grieve openly. The writer, Helen Franks, referred in particular to a report drawn up by a social worker who spoke of 'coffins smuggled through back entrances, bodies disappearing in plastic bin-liners'. She quoted, too, from a letter written by one of the members of staff in a residential home who said, 'Not letting other residents face the death of one of their number actually impoverishes them.'

The article conjured up a horrifying and sad picture similar to that envisaged by W E Henley in the lines:

Madame Life's a piece of bloom
Death goes dogging everywhere.
She's the tenant of the room,
He's the ruffian on the stair.

where death is seen as something to be feared and to be ignored wherever possible. But the underlying premise of the article – that death is a reality which has to be faced – is true not only for residents in homes for the elderly but for every single one of us.

As the silversmith in the Brother Cadfael mystery, *The Potter's Friend,* puts it so beautifully: 'We live as candles in the breath of God.' Death is inevitable sooner or later both for ourselves and for those about whom we care deeply, and we therefore need to see it, not as the end of everything, but as the fulfilment of the living which has preceded it.

Life is itself often a series of 'little deaths' and we shall be helped to come to terms with death more gently if we can learn to accept and work through the 'little death' experiences of loss which occur throughout our lives in one form or another.

Inevitably we are living with loss all the time and if we have the courage to recognise what is happening and to respond with determination and a sense of realism we shall know that loss can always result in growth and new life in spite of the pain which accompanies it.

* * * * *

It is never easy to die;
and yet we are always dying,
dying to what is so old and outworn
that it no longer houses us sufficiently.
Life is, after all, a succession of deaths;
the moving out from a place
for which we no longer hold the tenancy
to a new country or a new home.

If we are wise enough to recognise
the moment of departure . . .
the loneliness of that hour
when we must leave behind
the life which for one reason or another
is no longer possible . . .
if we can bear to look death in the face,
confront our fears,
our aching doubts as to whether or not
there is anything on the other side,
we shall arrive . . .
in a place not of our choosing perhaps
but always familiar;
where old hopes, old friends, faces we knew and loved,
experiences we tried to hold within our grasp
for too long . . .
will all converge into that single, shining point of time
which is eternity.

but first, there is death.

Joan Farrow

This poem captures the essence of my faith about death. Part of our life as Christians is to learn to be at home with our dying. Of all people we should be able to face death with expectation and with trust, however saddened we may be at the thought of the inevitable partings it involves both from people and from the finite things of beauty and worth which have given us so much immense pleasure and joy during our lifetime.

When people I love have died it is the little 'jewel' moments of life that I am sad they are going to miss – Janet, who died before I could take the first snowdrops from her garden to her in hospital and Norman, who died the week before his daughter's wedding; my father, who died at the age of 39 and Felicity, who took her own life at 22, both of whom missed so much through dying so young.

It's difficult to come to terms with the fact that life can be so beautiful and yet so fragile and that, as physical beings in a natural world which arouses and delights the senses, we are inevitably going to find that eyesight fades, hearing becomes hard, memory less good and that finally we apparently lose touch with all that has made life worth living in the physical dimension.

Yet if God has given us so much of beauty and imagination, colour and variety in this world, what possibilities that opens up for the next! We need to 'face death' together in a more accepting and practical way and to try always to approach it in terms of resurrection.

We live in time now, but we are destined for eternity. Jesus made light of death in many ways. In fact, for him, death itself seemed scarcely to be an issue. He was as vulnerable as we are to the pain that can accompany death, but he knew that, in the end, his Father would never forsake him, and as we journey through life to the point where the candle finally flickers and goes out, we, too, can know the same certainty. But we shall only know that certainty if we have learned how to live so that our preparation for facing death is actually happening all the time as we learn to face life.

Bereavement

We have learned to bury our deaths
Stifling their pain within ourselves
Whilst struggling at all costs
To keep a bright façade
And tear a blind across our agonies
Have known our solitude in grief
As second death
Almost as hurtful as the first
And just as hard.

There is, in any case, no spelling out for others
The clenched and aching hurt that follows loss,
As memories come flooding back and all the times
Of trust and happiness are etched
Upon our heart and mind as clear
As if the person cared for still drew breath.

The grief we keep inside can cause a wound
Too sharp for healing.
Yet what chance have we whose tears go deep
And cannot always be contained
Within acceptable convention
To mourn sufficiently
And weep our grief in company and comprehension?

Our grief today is not designed to show.
Mourning is limited and life goes on,
As we go on, smothering death
Under a flippant cloak.
We try to close our senses to the pain
And lightly say, 'She died, you know,'
Whilst inwardly we, only, meet our need.
We put our arms around ourselves –
And weep.

And yet we understand a better way.
Our grieving should not be so circumscribed.
We are not islands, but we are all made
Part of the main, diminished each by death.
Enriched, too, by each life that has been led.
Therefore our grief is open to relief
If we can trust enough to share our pain.
We need the touch of tenderness and care
The words of hope, the comfort of our friends.
We need to weep in other people's arms,
To vent our anger and our disbelief,
To speak our hurt and recognise our loss
Rather than cradle death within ourselves.

This is the lesson we must learn
Knowing that scars begin to heal
When those who live are friends in death
And carry compassion to our need.
If we can learn to let our friends
Hold both our past and present in their arms,
Then we can let the future in
Negotiating step by step
Along the strange, sad path of grief,
Feeling the pulse of hope revive
As others journey by our side.
Tears wept alone do have a place
But tears we share are gifts of grace.

Ann Bird

Learning to die means no longer to hate or be burdened with fear. To learn to die means to be caught up in a great chorus that affirms life; that is what faith is.

The more we learn to live in freedom from fear the more we learn to die in freedom from fear. The more we are united to that love with which we know ourselves to be at one, the more immortal we are. As Christians we know that death always lies behind us; it is love that lies ahead.

Dorothee Soelle

When we are dead and people weep for us and grieve, let it be because we touched their lives with beauty and simplicity. Let it not be said that life was good to us, but, rather, that we were good to life.

Jacob Rudin

CARE-LESS WORDS?

Saying 'No'

It would be fascinating, if it were possible, to programme a computer to produce a list of all the words we use in a particular month. If the computer were then able to tell us how many times we had used each word we should probably learn a great deal about ourselves and our priorities!

Certainly for those of us who write or speak about the pastoral ministry of the Church I suspect there are certain words that would appear with great regularity – words such as loving, friendship, acceptance, sensitivity and vulnerability. There's nothing wrong with that, we might say, although if those were the only 'pastoral' words to appear we might begin to wonder whether we were not becoming just a little too bland in our expression and practice of pastoral care. And if we take seriously the belief that pastoral care relates to the whole of people's lives we might look back at our list to discover which words, that perhaps ought to be there, rarely appear!

Our choice of words is surely determined by our view of pastoral care. It is easy to see our caring as concerned only with befriending people in their suffering and difficulty and to ignore the sharper edge of caring involvement which can enable people to grow and to enjoy fulfilment. Of course we need to be accepting of others, to be non-judgmental, to listen to them and to pray for them, to be prepared to receive as well as to give, to be loving. But in order to be flexible and able to respond to people at all their different levels of experience and need we cannot totally ignore some less obvious approaches signified by words which can, in the right context, be as full of care as those already mentioned.

I should like to see words such as honesty, discipline, morality, ethics, justice, coming up on my computer list from time to time, not to mention the three words laughter, failure and anger which are looked at in more detail later. And I should want to see the little word 'no' used in a pastoral context. I would guess that most of us find 'no' one of the hardest words to say. 'Yes' trips off the tongue much more easily and then often lands us in situations with which we are unable to cope.

We become caught between believing that God is expecting us to be totally self-sacrificing and knowing that we have our own limitations of time and energy. Michel Quoist sums it up all too clearly –

> – we are doing only one tenth of what we can see we should be doing,
> – we are only doing one-hundredth of what we could do if only . . .
> – we are only doing one-thousandth of what we would like to do.

I'm sure Jesus felt as we do, hemmed in and pressurised by people's needs; but when he became overwhelmed by it all he took himself off. He went away from people for a while and we ought to have the courage and the sense to do the same. Perhaps common sense should be another of the words to ponder. No one person can care for everybody. We have to say 'no' to some situations. And we do well to remember what Jesus said about the vine and the branches. Each one of us is, after all, only one branch. We are not expected to do everything and care for everybody. It is the quality of our care that is of particular importance.

I remember someone once saying to me – 'If you really don't have time to do something, what makes you so sure that God wants you to do it?' Perhaps 'no' is a more pastorally 'careful' word both for ourselves and others than we have sometimes realised.

Laughter

I remember the first time I went to a family funeral being totally taken aback by the joking and laughter that went on after we had all returned to the house for a meal. It seemed unfeeling and out of place and I was really quite upset by it at the time. Now, of course, I realise how necessary laughter can be in that kind of situation as a means of releasing tension and heartbreak. 'Humankind cannot bear very much reality' and a little light relief can sometimes make unbearable situations a little more bearable.

So let us not always be too serious in our expectations of pastoral care, for even in the most horrific situation laughter can break in as a sign of people's defiant refusal to be beaten by the circumstances in which they find themselves. Victor Frankl recounts how, even in Auschwitz, humour was one of the weapons in the fight for self-preservation. In fact, the prisoners frequently felt that laughter was the only weapon they had left to them.

Most of us fight shy of people who appear to have no sense of humour. We warm to those who can share a joke and who have the ability to laugh at themselves as well as, in kindly fashion, about other people. Laughter seems to make people more essentially human and if we find ourselves with people who cannot laugh at all we may well be with those who are in urgent need of the most sensitive caring ministry we can offer to save them from total despair.

Above all, humour and laughter in pastoral care introduce a sense of distance and perspective. By being able to 'see the funny side of a situation' we can, if only in small measure, rob it of its potential to overwhelm us completely, and sometimes the perspective provided by humour enables people to change and grow. Richard Boston in *The Anatomy of Laughter* has a lovely image of an oyster which underlines this:

We need laughter, just as we need love. Were we entirely rational without any hang ups, neuroses or tensions, then we would need neither. Laughter is like the pearl which the oyster forms around a speck of irritation. The entirely healthy oyster produces no pearls and the inhabitants of Utopia do not laugh. Laughter exists in an imperfect world, and it makes us rejoice that it is imperfect.

Laughter also has a great deal to do with acceptance. When we laugh at ourselves and when we laugh at other people without any malice we accept them. We laugh at ourselves because we are not perfect and when we smile as we make mistakes and do silly things we are accepting ourselves in a kind of loving forgiveness which reminds us of God's forgiveness – and not only of his forgiveness. Bishop George Appleton in his Easter Prayer suggests to us that laughter can also point us to the triumph of God's love in the Resurrection:

O risen Lord
    you must have laughed
when you went to Mary
    and she took you for the gardener
when you joined your friends
    on the country walk
    and they thought you a stranger
when you suddenly appeared
    in the room of remembrance
    and your companions
    feared you were a ghost.
Laughter of Easter joy!
    for something had happened
    a transformation, a transfiguration
space and time no limitation
    death no captor
    but a new dimension
your eager spirit released
    in universal presence
    visible to the eye of the spirit
Christ, we laugh with you
    on your great day and ours.

Failure

From childhood onwards most human beings in our culture seem always to be striving to achieve 'success' and, if we are not careful, even in our pastoral ministry we tend to feel we have to be 'successful' in terms of helping people and caring for them. But learning to deal with failure and learning through failure is an essential part of living and unless we come to terms with the fact that we are going to fail again and again we are in for a rough time. Maria Boulding, a contemplative nun at Stanbrook Abbey, reminds all would-be perfectionists –

> We fail because we are weak, wounded, confused and inconsistent. We each have particular built-in weaknesses, flaws that seem to be part of the very stuff of our characters. We fail to do and we fail to be. We fail in the good we try to do, and we fail to love. At the deepest level of our life is sin, we fail God.

Perhaps one of our greatest failures is our seeming inability to come to terms, not just with other people's failures, but with our own. It comes back once more to being able to accept people as they actually are rather than how we would like them to be and it has not a little to do with our needing to be able to laugh at ourselves.

If we are at all realistic about life, failure in pastoral care is inevitable. We are not always going to say the right words at the right moment, we shall no doubt offend some whom we are wanting to befriend, we shall misjudge situations and we shall be inadequate in all kinds of ways. But, having said that, it is only when we are able to live with our own ability to fail that we are really likely to be the kind of people with whom others dare share their failure.

Failure, in fact, goes right to the heart of being human. It heightens our sensitivity and compassion and enables far greater mutuality of caring to take place. And if we cannot cope with failing and being seen to fail we are not yet in a position to love and to be loved.

We have a good example before us. Christ himself was, in one sense, history's greatest failure and we do well to draw strength from the knowledge that he has gone down into the deepest places of our failure and claimed them as his own so that there is no possible failure in our lives or our deaths that cannot be the place of meeting him.

It is this that makes us sure that God is with us in all our pastoral ministry, in our 'success' and in our 'failure'. It is not even for us to judge which is which. We can only offer ourselves to others in love trusting that God will use our ministry in ways that make our reckoning of 'results' look foolish. The marvellous lesson to be learnt about Christian ministry is that it is not born out of skill or knowledge but that it springs from the experience of inadequacy, failure and rejection transformed by the love of God and then offered to others.

Two trees
proclaim in spring
a word to the world.

one exploding
into blossom
trumpets glory

one stretching
dead limbs
holds the empty
body of God

both speak
with due reserve
into the listening
ear of the world.

Ralph Wright

Anger

Anger does not immediately spring to mind as a word to be used in relation to pastoral ministry. We are afraid of anger, seeing it as destructive in terms of relationship and at variance with the desire to love people and to 'turn the other cheek'. But anger, if accepted as normal and handled with honesty, can actually become creative and liberating as Martin Luther knew when he wrote 'Anger refreshes the blood and sharpens the mind.' Martin Luther King, too, acknowledged anger as 'a precious and important commodity'.

This takes some believing for most of us. Words like 'sensitivity' and 'vulnerability' are much nearer the acceptable mark. We are all too aware that our own anger is not always the 'righteous' anger which seems to have Scriptural approval and, since we frequently become angry with those we love most, we are afraid to express our anger in case we put that love at risk. So we only allow ourselves to express 'good' feelings and feel uncomfortable and guilty about others and we forget that we are not primarily responsible for our feelings, only for what we do about them. And in the midst of all the tension we forget, too, that we are never more sensitive or more vulnerable than when we are angry.

Anger and hurt go hand in hand. We can be hurt in so many ways; hurt by being misunderstood; hurt by being neglected; hurt on behalf of those we care about – and such hurts inevitably involve deep feelings of anger. What we need to discover is how to handle our anger and that involves honesty and courage as we check that the source of our anger is not simply a sense of personal outrage but a serious concern for good relationships or social justice.

Anger after a bereavement is a recognised stage in the grieving process and the expression of such anger in the company of an understanding friend can become a part of the liberating, healing process. The final speech in the play *Shadowlands* is a cry of anger and grief on the part of C S Lewis as he struggles to make sense of a loving God who can allow people to suffer as his wife, Joy, has done, but the audience are left in no doubt that Lewis has a greater understanding of God as he expresses anger and loss than he has glimpsed before within his calm, anger-less academic world.

Anger, though, is not only necessary in helping people to gain greater insight and emotional maturity. It can also be truly liberating both for individuals and for society. Stevie Smith's poem 'Anger's Freeing Power' tells of a pet raven encouraged to fly from its three-walled prison. It remains in its self-imposed captivity until two fellow ravens make it so angry by mocking its stupidity that it escapes its prison.

> And in my dream I watched him go
> And I was glad, I loved him so,
> Yet when I woke my eyes were wet
> To think Love had not freed my pet.
> Anger it was that won him hence
> As only Anger taught him sense.
>
> *Stevie Smith*

So in our pastoral ministry we need to deal with anger – ours and other people's – in such a way that it will help people to escape from the 'prisons' of depression, hostility and injustice which oppress us all in one way or another.

We can, in fact, be too 'nice' and the effect of 'chronic niceness' can be to diminish both ourselves and our fellows who suffer as a result of our inability to protest in an articulate and often politically effective manner on their behalf. So, as long as we never allow anger to become a weapon against others, we can see it as a means by which people can on occasion be helped to be more free, and through which we can establish more honest relationships with each other. George Herbert and St Paul have much to teach us about anger!

> Ah, my dear angry Lord,
> Since thou dost love, yet strike;
> Cast down, yet help afford
> Sure I will do the like.

I will complain, yet praise;
I will bewail, approve;
And all my sour-sweet days
I will lament, and love.

Putting away falsehood,
let everyone speak truth with his neighbour.
Be angry but do not sin;
do not let the sun go down on your anger.

Ephesians 4:25, 26

Anger, laughter, failure, no – these are all words which we might allow to come a little higher on our imaginary computer list in future. For if they are always used in a context of compassion they could enable us to be more 'care-full' in our pastoral ministry, more able to 'see life steadily and see it whole'.

ELEMENTS OF CARING

I concede that the four elements of earth, air, fire and water recognised by ancient and medieval philosophers are not concepts which seem immediately relevant to pastoral ministry, though I believe they can in fact provide us with fresh insights! I increasingly find that all kinds of unlikely images and words can lead me deeper into an understanding of what it means to care, so even to dwell on the word 'elements' itself for a space is no bad thing.

Element is a word which evokes various images for me. It conjures up first principles, essential ingredients, things which are, in a way, restricted and confined. And yet it contains, too, that sense of free-ranging, awesome power expressed in the words of the hymn 'the elements madly around thee are raging', where the elements that surround us are seen as hostile and menacing and where God as creator is present not only in the still small voice but also in the storm and tempest.

Most of us are all too well aware that as we receive and give care we are frequently caught up in this same paradox. We are comfortable with the acknowledged elements of caring, the essential principles of listening in love, acceptance, refraining from judgment, consistency, mutuality, availability, to name but a few. But we are less at ease about the confusion we feel as we try to care for those we do not understand or do not like, or for those whose experiences resonate so deeply with our own that we find it hard to withstand enough of our own pain and insecurity in order to help them cope with theirs. Both sides of the coin are real elements within our caring. Both have to be taken account of as we look at the elements of our own pastoral ministry, and it follows that an important element of our care has surely to be humble enough to know that we are not always going to get it right and that there are often other elements implicit in situations of which we may not be aware. We have to try, with the help and grace of God, to share both pain and joy with others in such a way that they glimpse God's love.

Earth

I realise that I am inviting you to stretch language and play with metaphor as I tease out meaning from the word 'earth' as an 'element of caring', but it can be helpful to look at the unlikely and unusual as an aid to pastoral understanding and insight.

Earth, I think, speaks to us of basics, of the 'down to earth' necessities of our everyday living. It reminds us that our care for others can border on the merely sentimental if we are not concerned about their physical welfare or about trying to respond to their fundamental needs. It serves, too, as a reminder of our common humanity, of the fact that we are 'of the earth, earthy' (1 Cor. 15:47) and that 'all are of dust and all turn to dust again.' (Eccl. 3:20). With such knowledge it seems incredible that we can allow race, cultural differences, nationality, class to divide us as we walk on common ground, eat food grown in the same earth, appreciate the beauty springing from the earth which is given for every one of us to see and to enjoy. As followers of an Incarnate God we are compelled to translate this common 'earthly' heritage into concern that does not allow us to tolerate inequality and injustice and which emphasises the equal value of each individual in such a way that we are prepared to fight for what is right in social and political action.

On a more homely level I find a great deal of pastoral imagery can be discovered in the task of gardening. It is salutary as I am kneeling on the ground, for example – and such kneeling is in itself a powerful image of reverence for others – to look at the various pebbles in the earth. There are such different sizes, shapes, colours – so reminiscent of the infinite variety to be found amongst women and men – even a reminder of our differences in personality and of the fact that, however angular or dominating or insignificant we may find people, they all have their own identity, their own place in God's creation and are, therefore, precious.

But it is not only pebbles and earth I see when gardening. I delight as well in the variety of the flowers, the freshness of leaves, the sight of little green shoots amid the brown earth – even the weeds are beautiful in their proper element! All of these can evoke the picture of beauty coming from darkness, of hope and new life springing from what at first appears dead and barren. And we, too, in our caring can perceive the possibility of new life and fresh opportunity as we share our belief that even in times of loss or despair or just the mundane earthiness of life, people can discover signs of new beginnings and renewal if only they have eyes to see.

Elizabeth Barrett Browning knew this to be true as she expressed in her marvellous lines

> Earth's crammed with heaven,
> And every common bush afire with God;
> But only he who sees, takes off his shoes,
> The rest sit round it, and pluck blackberries.

If we want to 'see into the life of things', see into the heart of our pastoral ministry, we need to 'take off our shoes' in the presence of any image that can make us more aware of our common humanity and more sensitive in all our dealings with other people. Only thus can we offer God's love in all its fullness and variety.

It is not more wonders that we need but more wonder.

John V Taylor

Air

In *Stories and Prose Poems*, Alexander Solzhenitsyn speaks of the single most precious freedom that was denied to him in his imprisonment – the freedom to breathe. Once released he revelled in his ability to breathe freely and testified 'As long as there is fresh air to breathe under an apple tree after a shower, we may survive a little longer.'

Much of our pastoral ministry is concerned with helping people to 'survive a little longer' and to offer them 'freedom to breathe' in a metaphorical sense. So many are imprisoned by circumstances or by personality, by fear or by need of one kind or another, and it frequently seems difficult for them to relax into life and 'breathe' normally. As Christians we are caught up in trying to make the rhythm of life natural and comfortable for others so that they are not deprived of the necessities of life and so that the air breathed is not poisoned with hurt and unkindness, with injustice or neglect, let alone contaminated in the more tangible sense of polluted atmosphere.

Earth, air, fire and water are traditionally symbols of life and our ability to enjoy and use them as intended has much to do with our quality of life. Perhaps, therefore, we need frequently to remind ourselves that, in order to care for many in our society today, we have to concern ourselves far more radically with ensuring that their quality of life not only takes for granted the basic necessities of food and water, shelter and warmth but that it also gives them the freedom to be truly themselves. The phrase 'free as air' is not without its desperate poignancy for many people today, and in the same way that air has no frontiers so neither should our caring for others be restricted in any way. We want freedom for all – freedom with responsibility, yes – but 'freedom to breathe' in its fullest sense.

Those of us who suffer from asthma and who literally do not always have freedom to breathe are particularly aware of how precious is the element of air that is so often taken for granted. Of the four elements it is the most intangible and yet it is the most fully present element for all of us. Because it is our natural element, air is necessary for life itself. We need it to give us energy. We need it to nourish us and fill our lungs and bodies and make us what we are. And in the same way we need the 'air', the breath and spirit of God in our lives to give us energy, to make us fully human, to infuse everything that we do and everything that we are. As we care for others in all the neighbourly, practical and social ways that are so important, we must never allow ourselves to forget our total dependence on God's breathing His Spirit into all we try to do. Only as we allow ourselves to breathe in this love as naturally as we breathe in the air around us are we ourselves free enough to share His love and freedom with others. Then we shall know the truth of the words:

> There's a spirit in the air,
> Calling people everywhere:
> 'Praise the love that Christ revealed,
> Living, working in our world.'
>
> Still the Spirit gives us light
> Seeing wrong and setting right;
> God in Christ has come to stay;
> Live tomorrow's life today.

> *Brian A Wren*

Fire

When St Paul and his companions landed on the island of Malta they were treated with 'uncommon kindness' by the islanders, who lit a bonfire to provide them with both warmth and welcome. The whole episode, described in Acts 28, is a marvellous example of hospitality – especially with that word's true meaning of 'love of the stranger' – and through the centuries a fire has frequently been a symbol of warmth and hospitality, the place around which families and friends have gathered, where sharing of news and food has taken place, and where people have felt safe and valued.

It is not difficult, therefore, to see fire as an 'element' where care is natural and where individuals and groups feel at home and at peace with the world and with one another. But such is life that the warmth and happiness of others often emphasises the misery of those who are unable for one reason or another to experience such good things for themselves, and as carers we need to be aware of this and make sure that we are never exclusive in our caring. The lonely and the difficult also need the warmth of friendship and family life, and the homeless, above all, need the 'fire' which provides not only companionship but physical warmth and food, so we need to be 'fired' with determination not to allow either ourselves or society to neglect those who do not enjoy these basic necessities as a right.

However, fire is not only warming, it is also cleansing and purifying and it may be that sometimes our caring ministry has also to be 'fiery' in nature as our justifiable anger is directed against thoughtlessness and injustice and all situations where we can see that people are left out in the cold either literally or metaphorically. There is power in fire as well as warmth and both are necessary as we seek to be kingdom people who have a burning desire to ensure that no one is without heat or shelter or a friend to give the warmth of companionship.

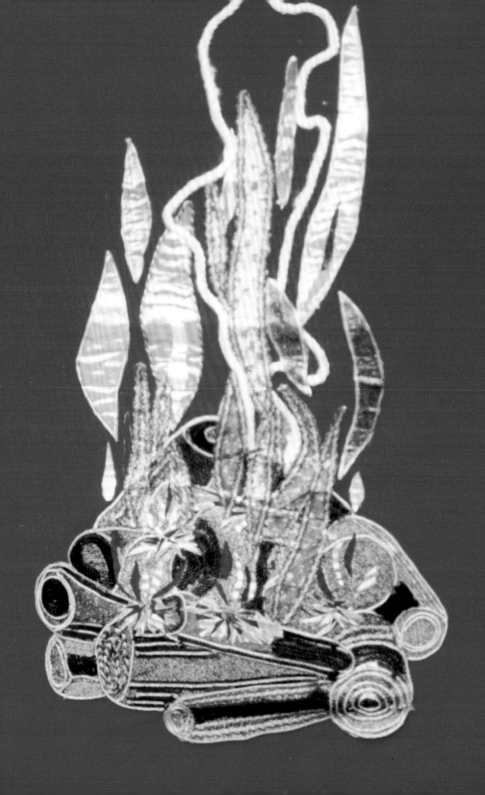

There are truths, too, that we can learn from the ever-changing movement and light that are visible in the flames of a fire. Life itself never stands still and one of our tasks as we befriend others is to help people to come to terms with change. Loss and change are an integral part of existence, but they are not always easy to negotiate and we need to be patient with those whose experiences have burnt into their consciousness in such a way that they are bitter or resentful or, simply, very sad. At such times our warmth and understanding, our own 'hospitality' in terms of welcome and acceptance, offered freely and consistently, will mean more than many words and well-intended phrases.

Brightness is another important facet of fire and caring is about the bright side of life as well as the dark. If we only react to people's need and never celebrate their gladness we shall not be caring in the fullest sense. We should naturally 'rejoice with those who rejoice' as well as 'weep with those who weep' and the most colourful of the four elements serves as a reminder that life is meant to be exciting, vivid and joyful.

It should also remind us that the Pentecost experience was expressed in 'tongues of fire' and that our pastoral ministry must always allow God's spirit and grace to be expressed through us. It is God who offers hospitality and welcome, warmth and power to us all, the cared for and the carers, and, if we will let him, he will stir the embers of our often inadequate efforts to care so that the steady glow of his love will inflame and irradiate all that we do in terms of pastoral ministry.

Water

Water, the fourth 'element', has very natural affinities with pastoral care. We have only to recall the words in Matthew 25 where Jesus speaks of giving a drink to those who are thirsty or 'the cup of cold water' referred to earlier in that gospel to realise how important it is to respond to each other's human needs. However, water is at such a premium in so many areas of the world today that we cannot simply concern ourselves with practical acts of kindness and concern in our own neighbourhood and society; we have to be actively engaged in bringing pressure to bear on those who have the power to share the earth's resources in a more equitable fashion for the benefit of all.

In a more metaphorical sense we can see our pastoral ministry as a way of helping to calm troubled waters. We frequently find ourselves involved in attempting to become channels of peace in this way as we listen quietly to whatever others may need to say to us. In her biography of Cicely Saunders, Shirley du Boulay quotes an Hasidic question and answer which contains wisdom for all listeners:

> Why do you say you should listen to someone as if you were looking on water rather than as if you were looking in a mirror?
> Because you have to be very still if you are going to see in water, you can so easily disturb it.

Our inner stillness, a stillness which is reflected not only by our body but also by our spirit, is very important for those who are needing our attention. Such serenity is not something which we acquire without discipline and humility or without coming to terms as far as possible with our own pain and hurt. Moreover some personalities will obviously find this easier to achieve than others. But we can all become more peace-full people if we let the spring of our care for others arise from our own dependence on God. If we immerse ourselves in his unfathomable love we shall have living water to offer to others.

On the other hand, if we allow ourselves to become parched and dry there will be nothing much left to flow freely to others.

O strengthen me, that, while I stand
Firm on the rock, and strong in thee,
I may stretch out a loving hand
To wrestlers with the troubled sea.

To neglect the cleansing properties of water would be to miss another important pastoral image. As carers we are called to be reconcilers, to encourage the free flow of forgiveness between people. And we are called, too, to help people to see themselves and the situations which cause them pain more clearly, even, maybe, to help them to feel clean and whole again. We are not just good neighbours, concerned with giving and receiving practical help, important though that is. We also have the water of life to offer others as we share with them our own belief (however thin a trickle that belief may seem to us at times) in the overflowing love of God to all the human race. It is when our own thankful response to God's love wells up in us and spills into everything that we do and are that we are able to reflect that love in our caring as water reflects the image caught in its light.

So often I find that my own care for others fails to spring from a dependence upon God's unfailing love and enabling power. The poem on the following page expresses my frustration with my own lack of faith and my longing to allow myself to rest more completely in the centre of his love.

Why do I stay
Circling the edges of desire,
Slaking my need for you
In things, which, good themselves,
Bring no relief?
I cannot tear myself
Free from your grace
Nor ease my longing
With a shift of heart.
Such yearning's part of me,
A cutting edge in all I do.
In all I think and feel,
In all I have become
And I would have it so
With all the pain it brings
For I can only find myself
Within my search for you.

I count the moments when I feel your touch
And greet their preciousness
As gifts so good
That they alone
Should constitute
A lifetime's certainty
Attracting me to you.
But all the while
My drawing back onto the outer edge
Denies experience
Belies my need
Speaks of my lack of trust.
Drawn by the magnet of your love
Still I seek refuge
In periphery
Fearing commitment
As I fear your love.

Oh my most patient, gentle God,
The circle's edge is not my home
Though I still live on it.
It is the centre that I crave

Where all is drawn together
In sheer grace, where peace
And consummation are the norm.

When will I learn to free my wayward self
My yearning and my longing
And my deep felt needs
From the circumference
On which I dwell
Into that different place
Where all **is** well?

Ann Bird

* * * * *

All the four elements that we have thought about have their own place in God's creation and all contain within themselves infinite variety. Our ministry of care, too, is composed of many elements but as we, too, are many different people having different insights and gifts to offer to each other, so it is this diversity which opens up the opportunity for us to be truly creative in our caring as we seek to become channels of God's love so that it can stream out to others in this marvellous world.

MEDITATIONS FOR ADVENT
AND CHRISTMAS

These five meditations on particular words or themes connected with Advent and Christmas are intended to help us to see our preparations and celebrations in the perspective of the light of Christ rather than in the context simply of our own immediate concerns.

Advent

The season of Advent is traditionally a time of anticipation and expectation and of preparation for the coming of God into our world. That, at least, is the liturgical understanding of this season in the Christian year. But for most of us such anticipation all too easily becomes an ideal rather than a reality as we become so pressured with preparation for Christmas festivities and so overwhelmed by the commercialisation of it all, that we have little space left for anything other than concerns which have little or nothing to do with the breathtaking fact of the birth into this world of the Son of God. In the words of W S Beattie

These are the greedy days.
It used to be
That Advent was a longing fast,
A time to feel our need
In faith and tingling hope
And keen-eyed looking forward.
Now we cannot wait
But day by day and week by week
We celebrate obsessively
Clutching at Christmas.
When at last it comes,
The day itself,
Our glass is empty.
We have held the feast
Already, and the news is stale

Before it ever reaches us.
We cheat ourselves.
Yet – somehow – still we hope
In these spoiled days
That there may be a child.

Mary prepared for the birth of Jesus 'in faith and tingling hope'. She did not prepare for the occasion in an obsessive, materialistic fashion. Instead, in what must have felt a very lonely way, she not only 'expected' a child but expected God's promise to be fulfilled through her in ways she could never have fully comprehended. And as we approach Christmas we are missing out on tremendous possibilities if we, too, are not preparing ourselves to expect God to come more fully into our lives regardless of the consequences.

For Advent should not simply be a time of waiting and of hope but also a time of immense challenge. It was certainly so for Mary. As we read and re-read the story of the woman who gave birth to Jesus it is inevitable that we lose much of its original impact. We know what happened. We know that Mary was all right. And we gloss over the pain and uncertainty of childbirth, the primitive circumstances, not to mention the fact that in the law of Mary's day the penalty for a betrothed woman being pregnant was death. Yet in spite of all the difficulties facing her, Mary, trusting in a God who was not yet incarnate, was prepared to say with immense courage – 'I am the Lord's servant. May it be as you have said.'

We certainly need to wait in quiet hope and expectation, as Mary did, but we need to do so not simply for our own sakes. We **do** know the reality of the incarnation. We should have some inkling of the challenge that it brings. Mary waited in expectation believing that God was using her to bring new life to the world around her, clearly a cause for joy and celebration and delight in new beginnings. But, having given birth, she was not left long in doubt that her joy was always going to be mixed with pain and a perpetual giving of herself in order that others should find blessing and healing. So Mary herself did not 'clutch at Christmas' in the sense of trying to keep the wonder and joy of it all to herself. Rather she 'let go' in a loving dependence upon God and in the knowledge that this Birth was vital to all people not simply to an immediate and 'chosen' circle.

Therefore our Advent expectation has to include such knowledge and our Advent hope cannot escape the kind of challenge that makes us translate Oscar Romero's words from Latin America into our own society and situation.

Advent should admonish us to discover
In each brother or sister that we greet,
In each friend whose hand we shake,
In each beggar who asks for bread,
In each worker who wants to use the right to join a union,
In each peasant who looks for work in the coffee groves,
      the face of Christ.
Then it would not be possible to rob them,
to cheat them,
to deny them their rights.
      They are Christ,
and whatever is done to them
Christ will take as done to him.
This is what Advent is:
Christ living among us.

Oscar Romero

Candles

Candles have had a tremendous impact on my own spirituality in terms of symbol and sign of God's presence. Through the lighting of candles as an accompaniment to intercession I have become increasingly aware of the way they can link people in prayers across great divides, and through watching the purity and brightness of their flames I have at times caught glimpses of the purity and brightness of God. So I cannot bring myself to talk of words associated with Christmas without sharing something of my love of candle-light, especially since Christmas is above all the time when we celebrate our knowledge that 'the light shines in the darkness and the darkness has never put it out.'

The light that shines in the darkness is in no sense simply an abstract light, nor is it just a kind of shining demand imposed on us that we should be good to each other. It is a vibrant, changing light that infuses the world with warmth and which penetrates into the dark places of our lives renewing us and giving us hope for the future. It is a light that we welcome although it brings challenge as well as illumination –

> Like a candle flame on a moonless night,
> Cheerily defying the darkness around,
> Jesus come to us as the Light,
> A light to lighten our darkness,
> The light of the World
> *Michael Brown*

Yet while we make huge claims for 'the light that shines in darkness', we do well to remember what an apparently little light it was in the first place. Candles too are little lights, yet each candle's light can have a wide effect on its surroundings. In the same way we too, in our own small way, can be a glowing reality of the love of God for others.

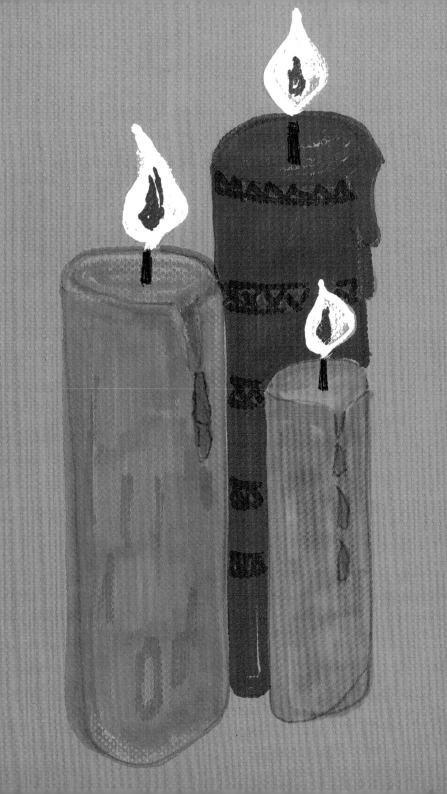

But as with all Christian symbols we have to be careful not to sentimentalise it. Light is vulnerable as well as powerful. Light is revealing, candles can burn, flames can easily flicker or be extinguished. Perhaps this is why in many places of the world candles have become the sign of protest or of solidarity – a social or political statement of courage and desire for cleansing.

> A candle-light is a protest at midnight,
> It is a non-conformist
> It says to the darkness
> I beg to differ.
>
> *Samuel Rayan*

A story from Chile vividly illustrates the power of such candle-light. On September 4th 1984 a priest was shot by a policeman in La Victoria. The news spread rapidly kindling emotions in the shanty town. Anything could have happened but some people had the idea of expressing their feelings by placing lighted candles in the trees and in the streets. Gradually more and more candles appeared, brought by people who lit their candles as a symbol of their shared longing for peace. For hours, La Victoria, normally a violent area, became the oasis of peace its inhabitants longed for.

The experience of Sally Hogan, a Methodist in South Africa is another testimony to the power of candle-light.

> My sister had just been moved from the long and terrible months of solitary confinement in detention to a prison to begin preparing for her trial. That day the candle burned as a symbol of our watching and praying with Barbara. Her suffering and that of many South Africans has not yet ended but a candle has been lit . . .

Since those words were written the situation in South Africa has changed dramatically and for all of us that is a source of immense joy and thankfulness. But it is still true that for thousands of people across the world candles are a sign of hope. They are also a sign of new life and of purification. In some Christian churches on the last day of Christmas there is a Candlemas service. As the worshippers come in each one is given an unlighted candle. Then at the close of the service the priest lights a candle from the altar. The servers light their candles from his and as the light from these candles is passed throughout the congregation one to another the whole church gradually fills with light. If such candle-light can transcend the symbolism so that we as candle-bearers can bring light into the world each Christmas maybe we shall help that world to understand more fully the truth that the light shining in the darkness can never be extinguished.

> In the word made flesh,
> God had sent his last word,
> his most profound word,
> his most beautiful word
> into the world.
> And that word means:
> I love you,
> world and humanity.
> Light the candles!
> They have more right here
> than darkness.
>
> *Karl Rahner*

Presents

In John Betjeman's poem *Advent 1955* are words which sound sickeningly familiar to us today.

> Some ways indeed are very odd
> By which we hail the birth of God.
> We raise the price of things in shops,
> We give plain boxes fancy tops.
> And lines which traders cannot sell
> Thus parcell'd go extremely well.
> We dole out bribes we call a present
> To those to whom we must be pleasant . . .

Not perhaps the greatest of poetry but food for thought about what we really mean by our Christmas giving to others. In contrast I think the gift that Robert Lee of South Carolina sent to his daughter on Christmas Day 1861 probably conveyed far more of his love for her than do many of our gifts today to the people about whom we care.

> I can only send you a little money but I send you, too, some sweet violets that I gathered for you this morning while covered with dense white frost, whose crystals glittered in the bright sun like diamonds, and formed a brooch of rare beauty and sweetness which could not be fabricated by the expenditure of a world of money.

However, I must not be hypocritical! I am an inveterate Christmas gift shopper and enjoy receiving gifts as much as anyone else does, but I also really enjoy trying to find the right present for those to whom I give. It takes time but I believe it is important and I also believe that Christmas is often the occasion on which to give something which is light-hearted, frivolous or even totally unnecessary! God's gifts around us speak of His lavish generosity, his love of variety and indeed of his sense of fun, and I think that to recognise this in our giving is all a part of celebrating his birthday. I am absolutely sure that God wants us to enjoy ourselves.

Where I am uncomfortable with myself, though, is in the knowledge that in a world which is full of such terrible deprivation and loneliness I, on the whole, give to those who already have, whilst paying scant attention to those in real need of whatever kind. We know that our Christmas present giving is frequently only a microcosm of our material spending and giving during the rest of the year. Yet we are all aware that there are no easy answers to the injustice and poverty in our own society, let alone in the world in general. It is so difficult to get the balance right between caring for, and giving to, those we know and reaching out to those who are in most need of our loving, practical understanding. Clearly, though, in the light of Bethlehem and God's generous and incredible gift of himself to his world we can never afford to become complacent about the tensions or to stop struggling with the issues in realistic fashion, however overwhelming the difficulties appear to be.

Perhaps we must be careful in the affluent west not to behave like the Romans who pandered to the greed of their emperor, Caligula, who, one New Year's Day, announced that he would stand out on his porch to receive gifts of money. If the sum received was not enough, the giver would be publicly shamed. Are we, too, guilty of trying to impress with our presents? Giving the most to those who need least? Or are we aware at Christmas of those who have little or nothing? for whom a well-chosen gift would be received as a special blessing, a sign that they are of value and remembered in the midst of all our busyness.

In terms of money the first Christmas was a very humble affair – in Betjeman's words –

> A present that cannot be priced
> Given two thousand years ago.

What God gave was himself, and the most precious gift we can give to others is the gift of ourselves in whatever appropriate form that giving may take.

Hugo Rahner had the right idea when he said that every Christmas gift should be a symbol of our love, every present 'like a sacrament, a making visible of an invisible good that goes further than our calculations, has no boundaries and recognises no frontiers', so that, 'however poor we may be, so poor that we have, in the weeks before Christmas, to go past the shop windows and their glorious displays of gifts perhaps with a troubled, hurt, and even envious heart, we can still say to those we love: "I give you my heart. My heart, my loving heart, is like a carefully locked Christmas present. It contains treasures that have still not been discovered. My love is new and full of surprises. It looks forward to receiving a gift in return. And it is renewed and made young again when it hears the only possible answer – I love you too."'

Signs of Incarnation

For the shepherds the signs of Incarnation were the light of the glory of God, the song of the angels and the message of peace and goodwill for all people. Those unsuspecting men were suddenly surrounded by the radiance and joy of God and so great was the impact upon them that, without hesitation, they responded to the vision they had seen and ran searching for the Baby of which the angel had spoken.

I can still vividly recall my own reaction to bending low in the cramped, rough-hewn cave we were shown in the Shepherds' Fields outside Bethlehem and feeling transported back to that moment of Incarnation as I looked out at the same landscape which the shepherds must have seen on that first Christmas Day. For me at that moment the sign of Incarnation was not so much of glory as of simplicity, of silence, and of an intense naturalness. Time seemed to telescope. Christ's birth became more focused in reality, and the ordinariness of it all made the original event even more extra-ordinary and immediate than it had ever seemed before. It had actually happened. A group of shepherds, ordinary people like me, had been suddenly stopped in their tracks and faced with God's presence in the world. The sign of Incarnation became real and demanding for me as it had done for the shepherds.

Less real for me was the visit to the Church of the Nativity where the floor of the 'cave' below the church is inset with a star, its silver worn away by kissing. This star is a reminder not only of the line of David but also of the star that was the sign of Incarnation leading the Magi to seek Jesus. But, in this context, it felt overlaid with too much splendour and, authentic as the place may be, I was conscious only of visual symbols rather than of the breathtaking awareness that the Word was actually made flesh at this particular spot on earth.

I often used to wonder why it was that only the shepherds and wise men saw the signs, the angels and the star, and why they were not visible to more people. But in fact it is evident that the essence of a vision is that it is seen only by those for whom it is intended. Sometimes the light of God's truth for us will flash upon us unexpectedly, a gift of grace, as happened for the shepherds; at other times we shall only see and recognise the meaning of the vision that is laid before us after study and preparation. The vision of the Wise Men was born out of their knowledge and understanding.

Signs of Incarnation lie all around us ready to be revealed by a loving God if we are receptive enough to respond to them and if we live in the expectation that God will speak to us in whatever way is appropriate. I expected to thrill with the immediacy of the moment at the place where Christ was born; I actually knew the presence of God in the hillside cave. I expected to feel deeply moved at his place of crucifixion and as I looked into the place of the sepulchre; the times when I met my Risen Lord were in the silence of a small boat on the lake of Galilee and walking on my own in the Garden of the Tomb where the words 'Ann, I am not here, I am risen' with all that they imply for **me, today,** rang deeply in my ears.

So if there is to be a special understanding for me at Christmas or if new light is going to be shed on my previous, present or future experience, that is in God's hands. All I can do is to offer him my love in openness and expectation and with humility so that it is possible for the Word made flesh to speak to me and touch my life as he touched the lives of the shepherds and the kings. I can also re-affirm my 'yes' to God and my desire to go from the place of Incarnation with him knowing that he will be on the journey from Bethlehem with me. And maybe I shall not see any particular new sign or hear any particular fresh word because the Sign of Incarnation has been made visible and been spoken to me already. Perhaps all that is asked of me is that I have the courage and faith to follow the signs that are already my Christmas gifts.

Christmas Past?

Well, so that is that. Now we must dismantle the tree,
Putting the decorations back into their cardboard boxes –
Some have got broken – and carrying them up into the attic.
The holly and the mistletoe must be taken down and burnt,
And the children got ready for school. There are enough
Left overs to do, warmed-up, for the rest of the week –
Not that we have much appetite, having drunk such a lot,
Stayed up so late, attempted – quite unsuccessfully –
To love all of our relatives, and in general
Grossly overestimated our powers. Once again
As in previous years we have seen the actual Vision and failed
To do more than entertain it as an agreeable
Possibility. Once again we have sent Him away,
Begging though to remain His obedient servant,
The promising child who cannot keep His word for long.
The Christmas Feast is already a fading memory,
And already the mind begins to be vaguely aware
Of an unpleasant whiff of apprehension at the thought
Of Lent and Good Friday which cannot, after all, now
Be very far off.

W H Auden

This is what we cannot allow to happen. The 'vision' we have seen at Christmas, albeit momentarily, is not just 'an agreeable possibility'. It is a God-given, radical imperative for all those of us who claim the name Christian. It is a vision of love and vulnerability that inevitably transforms the 'musts' and 'oughts' of life into a yearning, passionate desire to follow the star of Bethlehem wherever it may lead us. It is also about recognising that we shall fail to keep the vision of the Christchild, the Incarnate God, in our view if we imagine that we can do so in our own strength and without continual reliance on the God who has come among us to be with us in the way ahead.

So instead of allowing ourselves to feel tired and dispirited after all the excitement and the celebrations we need to give ourselves space to consider the meaning of Christmas for us as individuals.

If we have really allowed ourselves to hear the song of the angels, if we have looked into the face of the Christchild, if with the shepherds we have laid before him whatever is the appropriate offering for us, we shall have received from him far more than we can ever give. The trouble is we may not like what we have been given. We may regret that gift or the vision because to accept either would be too painful, too demanding for us and, after all, we have been here before. Most of us have celebrated Christmases and ended with the words 'So, that is that.'

But in one way or another, Christmas is only just beginning on December 25th for each one of us, for –

When the song of the angel is stilled,
When the star in the sky is gone,
When the kings and the princes are home,
The work of Christmas begins
    To find the lost
    To heal the broken
    To feed the hungry
    To release the prisoner
    To rebuild the nations
    To bring peace among people
    To make music in the heart.

Anon

When we thought about Advent, we talked of the way in which we can so easily 'clutch at Christmas', but as Mary Magdalene learnt in her meeting with the Risen Christ, we cannot 'clutch' at or restrain Christ in any one particular place or confine him to one particular occasion. He is the one who goes before us on the road from Bethlehem to Lent and Easter, to Calvary and Resurrection, and if Christmas has meant anything to us at all we have to join him on that road seeking the vision of his kingdom along the way and rejoicing in his incarnate presence.

73

WORDS OF FREEDOM

Acceptance

My faithful eight year old Renault 5 began to make it clear that if I continued to chase around the country in my usual fashion it would begin to cost me dear. So after much deliberation I settled on a replacement in the shape of a 5-door Nissan Micra automatic in a gorgeous metallic 'Arctic Blue'. I haggled my way to a good price and became quite excited at the prospect of owning what I visualized as the perfect car for my needs. Or that was the initial situation. Then a salesman telephoned me to say that I could have the said car in any colour but the one I wanted! Isn't he aware, I asked myself, that one of the main reasons for choosing the car in the first place was its alluring colour? By the time this appears in print I shall have decided whether to have the colour I want and settle for three doors, or a manual, or whether to start the wearisome process of choosing all over again; but when the salesman rang I was disappointed and frustrated that, as so often happens in life, I would have to accept second best when I had set my heart on what I saw as the ideal car for me.

Acceptance of this kind is, of course, trivial by any standards, let alone in comparison with the major issues which face us all on a repeated daily basis. On the other hand if we make a habit of seeing such unimportant 'acceptances' in perspective they can become stepping stones to the acceptance of larger potentially damaging situations which threaten to overwhelm us when we have to face them unexpectedly.

Life is not ideal or perfect and the more we expect it to be and refuse to accept its complexity and compromise the more we are likely to hurt other people and to be hurt ourselves. On the other hand there is inevitably going to be conflict for us in this area for we seem born to strive for that which is perfect and the resulting clash with reality when perfection persistently eludes us can cause a great deal of pain and discontent. The reality of this is never more evident than in our attitudes to our own character and personality.

From an early age we are taught that God accepts us as we are but we are also taught the doctrine of Christian perfection and we become confused by the knowledge that although we are called to 'be perfect' we are absolutely riddled with imperfections of all kinds, some of our own making and some implicit in our temperament or circumstances. Consequently – and in spite of the varied scholarly interpretations of the relevant New Testament texts concerning 'perfection' – in our heart of hearts we come to believe ourselves unacceptable to God and we see others as possessing gifts and graces that we covet and that we imagine make them more acceptable than we are ourselves. So we strive to be different, to be something other than ourselves and we try to earn acceptance by what we **do** rather than by what we **are,** and since this is not possible anyway most of us find it difficult or presumptuous to claim that we, too, share in Tillich's experience of knowing himself accepted –

> Sometimes a wave of light breaks into our darkness, and it is as though a voice were saying, 'You are accepted.
> You are accepted, accepted by that which is greater than you, and the name of which you do not know. Do not seek for anything, do not perform anything, do not intend anything. Simply accept the fact that you are accepted.'

I do not know of any foolproof way to know this for oneself other than to recognise it as a gift of assurance which God is longing to give each one of us, but I do know that it is a gift which, once given, is not taken away. My own moment of recognition came only comparatively recently whilst reading a book by Ronald Rolheiser called *The Restless Heart* when I was on a retreat at Launde Abbey. As I read a particular chapter I suddenly 'knew' – 'It's all right to be me' – and those words have stayed with me as both strength and affirmation. On many occasions since then it has felt anything other than 'all right to be me' and yet that experience has all the while been essentially liberating. However many times I inadvertently make mistakes, dislike myself, am disliked or misunderstood by other people, fall short of my own perfectionist goals, I know deep down that

God understands me and values me and loves me as I am. I, at last, accept that 'I am accepted'.

I have found, too, that this acceptance of myself not only helps me to sit more lightly to other people's expectations and opinions of me but it challenges me to be more gentle and gracious in my dealings with others. This has been reinforced by a recent experience of taking part in a Myers Briggs Retreat. Apart from helping individuals to look more closely at their own preferences such a Retreat provides a constructive way forward for relating to others and to God. It also heightens awareness and appreciation of difference and therefore gives renewed understanding not only of oneself but of all those who are very different from oneself and therefore sometimes very difficult to tolerate let alone love.

During the three day retreat we took part in various exercises which helped us understand why we all react so differently in similar or identical situations. It was deceptively easy to work with those whose 'personality-types' were like our own; planning a retreat garden with a group of like-minded 'extrovert, intuitive, feeling, judging' people (to use the 'jargon') was bliss; arguing one's corner in an imaginary church council meeting with an obstinate 'introvert, sensing, thinking, perceiving' person took every ounce of imagination and grace one possessed! But what a lot it taught me about the way in which we all approach life from different perspectives and with different abilities and perceptions and how much easier I have found it since to accept that any one person's experience and judgment is as valid and important as any one else's.

If we are to accept people in this way we are caring for each other as we really are, not as we would like one another to be. We are beginning to see people clearly, rejoicing in their uniqueness and acknowledging the authenticity of their experience whilst never denying the truth that we have come to know for ourselves. But acceptance of this kind is no easy option. Acceptance of ourselves and of others can be one of the most searching ongoing works of grace in which we are involved. It involves both a 'letting-go' and a 'taking-on' and the kind of spirituality of suffering and selflessness in which it often involves us has a very clear pattern and model in the theology of the cross.

Much of the time, however, our acceptance is concentrated on what appear to be predominantly practical issues, closely bound at all points with our pastoral concern and our relationships with each other on a daily basis. The reason for my wanting an automatic car is to make life easier for my husband whose left ankle and back were badly damaged in a car accident a few years ago. As someone who had always enjoyed sport and had numbered walking and gardening among his many hobbies he has had to accept severe physical limitations in recent years. We all have family and friends who have to live with similar frustrations through their own illness or handicap or the disability of those close to them. Many who are married have to work hard to accept behaviour which is hurtful or a relationship which only seems partially fulfilling; those who are single frequently have to accept loneliness; and all of us have to accept loss, disappointment and hurt on an everyday basis. Yet because fear of rejection also plays a significant part in our feelings of insecurity both about ourselves and with other people, we are unwilling to show ourselves to be vulnerable because we are afraid that if we do we shall be deemed unacceptable. So we tend to mask our wounds and hide our God-given uniqueness from each other and we fail to draw the strength we could from those around us who are themselves deep down eager to share something of their own humanity with those who will accept it.

In the end acceptance is about being real and about being realistic. Life is not perfect; we are not perfect; neither are those around us. As we seek to accept ourselves and other people we have to recognise that we cannot change circumstances very much but that we **can** change ourselves in that we can alter our reactions to what happens to us and to the way in which we behave towards the people to whom we relate. The most loving gift we can offer either ourselves or another person is the gift of acceptance, for within its wrappings come the accompanying gifts of love and gentleness and self esteem and peace of mind.

That is the kind of gift which is totally acceptable to us all, and it is one for which, when it is offered, we can only show our gratitude by accepting it gladly and without reserve.

Just before she died an old and valued friend wrote to my mother and ended her letter with the following observation:

> I have learned that most of life's graciousness can be summed up in three short words, 'Accept, Adapt, Adorn.'

They are good words for us all to remember for as we accept we learn to adapt and as we adapt to circumstances as they are for us we are more likely to 'adorn' the little bit of life that is ours in a way that speaks to others of the love of God.

* * * * *

For all that has been – Thanks.
To all that shall be – Yes!

Dag Hammarskjöld

All that I have ever heard or experienced
says this.
Those who love
are held together,
forever,
in the heart of Love.

But it is not always comfortable.

So know that you are held
in the heart of God.
Draw strength from that embrace.
Take courage.
This heart is Christ's gift to us.
Throbbing, pulsing with love,
of flesh, not stone.

In the sharing of our common hope,
our common pain,
we draw upon a well so deep
that none need go away thirsty.

In the sharing of our common prayer,
our common life,
we dip into a pool clear as glass,
strong as wine,
endlessly renewed . . .

So let love arise like a healing stream.
Pray the heart of Christ
into the void.
Hold the heart of love
in the wound of the world's pain
and know that the tears are seen, received,
shared, answered.

Julie Hulme

Forgiveness

> Love your neighbour **as** yourself
>
> Inasmuch **as** ye do it to the least of one of these . . .
>
> Forgive us our trespasses **as** we forgive those who trespass against us

Those 'as' sayings of Jesus are the ones that catch me out again and again. They trip off my tongue as lightly as anything until suddenly I realise I have been confronted with a situation about which I have to do something if I am ever going to read or say them again with a clear conscience. And that particular phrase in the Lord's Prayer about forgiving is the trickiest and most heart-searching of them all.

There are so many clichés about forgiveness which cheapen it and fail to recognise its true nature. 'Forgive and forget' we are advised, and in many instances of minor irritation or hurt this is perfectly possible and happens without any real cost to ourselves. But when we have been deeply hurt and our lives and relationships have been radically changed by that hurt we are simply adding another burden to the weight we are already carrying if we feel guilty because we are unable to brush aside the hurt and 'forget' it. Moreover, when we ourselves have been forgiven for a wrong or injustice done to someone else we are aware that it is precisely because the person concerned knows that we can behave in such a way and yet still loves and accepts us and wants to move forward in relationship with us that their forgiveness has such value. They accept us in spite of and including what has happened and in the giving and receiving of forgiveness we come closer together in understanding and friendship.

For most of us, whatever the circumstances, forgiveness is something that has to be worked at and is a process which continues for a long time. In its initial impact any deep injury to ourselves is a kind of bereavement and leaves us not only with similar feelings of pain and anger but also of deep insecurity.

Because of this, forgiveness is not a quick task which is over and done with once and for all. Rather is it a matter of living with a difficult situation and trying deliberately to feed constructive thought into it so that it begins to contribute to our growth rather than to detract from it.

We are unsure of ourselves at the best of times and if we are slighted or ridiculed or threatened in our significant relationships our fear and our hurt make us instinctively want to hit back or, at the very least, to defend ourselves against any further hurt. So it is all too possible for us either to hide behind a stoical acceptance of what has happened without making any moves about defusing the situation or to lash out in an attempt to inflict similar hurt on the one who has injured us.

Instead we have to realise that it is frequently our own anger and hurt we have to deal with not the injury itself; that has already taken place and nothing can be done about it. But in all situations where costly forgiveness is needed it is usually one's own anger, fear of rejection or insecurity that blocks the reconciling spirit.

We are fortunate if we have someone we trust with whom we can share our anguish because in the sharing itself there is healing. We are fortunate, too, if we have already tried within previous experiences to see the possibilities for growth which are present in every dark time. For becoming able to absorb injury and hurt is not a talent easily acquired at the actual time; rather it is a gift we are given as we try day by day to be gracious and positive about all the experience that comes our way.

Although it is not totally true to say that 'to understand all is to forgive all', it is a maxim that contains a surprising amount of truth. We are very conscious that the more we know about ourselves the more we understand our own reactions to events, so if we can become sensitive to the fact that everyone else is also conditioned by their own temperament, insecurity, fears and hopes we are a long way down the path of being able to understand why they have behaved as they have. Therefore we are more able to see our way to being able to forgive and to make a fresh start with them.

To pray for the person who has hurt us is intrinsic to our Christian conception of forgiveness and it cannot do other than transform the situation, although our prayer if it is to be real must include the anger and bewilderment and rejection that we feel as well as a desire for the other person's well-being. Certainly the prayer of forgiveness is a way of seeing that releases love, and intercession of this kind is, as Neville Ward says, 'faith seeing those who have wronged us, and ourselves, within the great reconciliation of God's kingdom and trusting our belief that he is at work to bring in that kingdom of truth and affection'.

We may be helped to pray in this way if we remember that it is within the occasions when we feel most distressed or perplexed that the kingdom of God is most particularly struggling and longing to break through for us. Our pain can, through the healing of prayer, become the pain of birth for all concerned.

So far the emphasis has been on our being able to forgive others but an even harder road for some of us is to ask forgiveness of others. There is a wise prayer for those who are married which reminds us all of our need to seek forgiveness as well as to offer it. 'Give them grace when they hurt each other, to recognise and acknowledge their fault and to seek each other's forgiveness and Yours.'

Most of us are involved in relationships which would be strengthened by a simple apology or a request for forgiveness, and it is salutary for us to remember from time to time that when we are unable to let go of the past and thus unable to forgive, our own identity can become defined by those whom we dislike and those who have hurt us. To ask for and receive as well as to offer forgiveness in the little exchanges of life as well as in its most wounding moments can only make us more accepting of each other and more acceptable to each other. Moreover it can only draw us into a closer relationship with the God who forgave even in the face of His own totally unmerited suffering.

Perhaps our greatest need for forgiveness arises from our many refusals to allow ourselves to grow both in our relationship with other people and with God. But if we ask for it in honesty and with a willingness to change our self-protective attitudes, God's forgiveness, freely offered to us, brings with it the grace and peace that make it possible for us to move forward in peace and freedom and the power to respond to and create new beginnings. God's forgiveness is marked by its gentleness and our forgiveness should mirror this. Carlo Caretto experienced this as he tells us –

> When, through my tears, I began to tell him (Jesus) something of the years during which I betrayed him, he lovingly placed his hand over my mouth in order to silence me. His concern was that I should muster enough courage to pick myself up again to try to carry on walking, in spite of my weaknesses, and to believe in his love in spite of my fears.

We too, in our relationships with others need, with God's help, to find the courage to carry on 'walking towards each other' offering and receiving forgiveness and believing that in doing so we are moving towards a deeper understanding of the healing and reconciling love of God.

I BEG YOUR PARDON

Easy for you to say 'Forgive'.
But how can I forget that hurt,
Welcome that person?
Etched deeply in my memory,
I can't 'forget' as though
It never happened.

Can I then learn to remember?

There is a way that keeps the hurt alive,
Quick to imagine other grievances.
There is a way that's based on a pretence –
That all was for the best – failing to
Realise the gravity of the event, or
Take it seriously. 'It doesn't matter',
Said dismissively, diminishes the person
Asking pardon, as well as failing
To acknowledge hurt.
There is a way that says. 'Yes,
That was bad, it hurt, but now,
In fuller knowledge of each other,
Let's go ahead and set each other free
To build up trust and grow again in love;
Perhaps together, but perhaps apart,
Only without the rancour that destroys.'

Ann Lewin

Affirmation

I have written earlier of our need to be able to say 'No' in situations where we are genuinely unable to offer help for one good reason or another or when we are so over-burdened ourselves that we have to recognise our limits of strength or vulnerability. But there is a much wider sense in which we need always to be saying 'Yes' to each other. This 'Yes' has nothing to do with our response to particular requests or our recognition of needs; rather it is a way of looking at every person we encounter in an attitude of positive acceptance, looking always for the good in them rather than latching on to their perhaps more obvious faults and failings.

We all respond to words of appreciation and encouragement with a lift of the spirit. Hearing such phrases as 'I do like your new jacket,' or, at a more profound level, 'I always come away from time with you feeling better,' we warm to the person who has taken time not only to notice us in some way but to express their enjoyment or appreciation of whatever it is that marked their attention. We go on our way feeling better for the encounter and more sure of ourselves.

We all need to be noticed and we all need to be taken seriously. I have an uncomfortable memory of taking my gentle and gracious 87 year old mother to see an eye consultant who, knowing that she suffers from all kinds of ills as well as being partially sighted, seemed to assume that she was also deaf and slightly stupid. Consequently he addressed all his carefully enunciated remarks to her in a loud patronising voice before discussing his real diagnosis with me in a much softer tone, totally unaware that she was listening to every word he said in her normal intelligent way. 'Do I take sugar?' she said with a smile as we shut the door behind us afterwards.

Her comment reminded me of a television interview I had watched when the commentator addressed all his remarks not to the boy, who though severely handicapped had just published a book of his own poetry and was perfectly capable of speech through an electronic device, but to the boy's parents. He never even looked at the boy once as far as I could tell.

Such failures in imagination and relationship occur all the time and are particularly cruel in relation to those who have to cope with disablement or deprivation of any kind. Perhaps it is no coincidence that the words about affirmation that have meant the most to me come from the pen of Jean Vanier, the founder of the L'Arche Community for those who have suffered the pain of rejection because of their handicap. Many who for a variety of reasons suffer injustice or rejection in our society today would assent to the truth of these words –

> By the power of affirmation
> people are led to trust in themselves
> and to discover their own beauty and riches.
> They realize they do not have to hide from others
> in anger and sadness.
> They are not dirty, ugly or evil.
> Through a caring, committed presence,
> people will discover
> > that they are allowed to be themselves;
> > that they are loved and lovable,
> > that they have gifts
> > and their lives have meaning,
> > that they can grow and do beautiful things.

There can be no greater pastoral calling than to be a 'caring presence' for another person, and we all need others who will be a 'caring presence' for us. We are all broken people, reaching towards each other through our own woundedness and heartbreak as well as through our experiences of joy and growth. And it is by means of our love and tenderness for each other, our appreciation and encouragement that we say the 'Yes' to one another that we all need so much to hear.

Knowing this as we do it is amazing how difficult we so often find it to put it into practice. As in our 'acceptance' of each other so in our attempt at 'affirmation' we can be so bound by our own sense of inadequacy, inferiority and insecurity that we tend to turn in on ourselves, seeking approval from others to bolster our own self-esteem rather than looking for moments where we can encourage and complement another.

Encouragement is a great 'affirmer'. Barnabas, given that name by the apostles because it meant 'Son of Encouragement', should be the patron saint and inspiration of all those of us who never want to lose sight of the importance of encouraging others. Emerson said that 'Our chief want in life is somebody who shall make us do what we can,' and it is very true that we discover unexpected abilities and possibilities within ourselves when we also discover someone who has faith in us. God affirms us in this way. We need to reflect that faith he has in us to one another as we see the best in each other and value and nurture each other's potential.

Some years ago I went to a workshop run by Bill Denning, a Methodist minister. Almost every one of us there began by saying 'I'm hopeless at anything artistic' and I **knew** that I was! But Bill accepted that that was how we all felt, he made no specious promises about our abilities but as he prepared us to enter into the creative experience as he talked about the walk to Emmaus, he awoke such an imaginative awareness within each one of us that we all set to with our clay, our painting or our poetry without any further belittling of ourselves.

For me that workshop was a liberating experience. My clay figures, in retrospect, were misshapen, childish and unimaginative but because I was encouraged and not ridiculed, because I was praised for what **was** good, not dismissed for all that was poor, because I had been treated with gentleness, courtesy and acceptance, I came away knowing that something deep inside me had been unlocked. It was no longer important that I was not 'good' at clay-modelling, embroidery, writing poetry, calligraphy. As long as I enjoyed trying to express myself through these media to the best of my ability that was all that mattered. Again it suddenly became 'all right to be me', as I said when writing about acceptance, and that in itself released me to be more sure of myself in the things I can perhaps do reasonably well. More than that, I am quite certain that I would not have been able to sustain my present work if it had not been for my encounter with Bill and the influence he had on me six years ago.

Sometimes in a workshop I ask people to choose a pebble that in some way represents for them a person who has been an influence for good in their lives. It is fascinating to discover how much we often learn together about our pastoral ministry in this way. Nearly always the person chosen is someone who has not only been consistent in their support and sensitive and honest in their dealings with the person concerned, they have also been those who gave encouragement and allowed people time to be themselves. We cannot do more for each other than say 'Yes' to each other's personality and gifts in such ways. It is amazing how many ripples spread from the one apparently insignificant 'pebble' thrown into the stream of our life.

It is sad that so often within the church community we say anything but 'Yes' to each other. I do not know how many ordained ministers survive when the rest of us are so quick to criticise rather than to affirm, so prone to judge rather than to encourage. None of us can be all things to all people. We all have our special giftedness and our particular contribution to make both to the church as the Body of Christ of which we are all members and to the world in which we all play our part. We give renewed life to each other by being loving and gentle with each other, by offering mutual appreciation and affirmation. People blossom when they are valued. We do indeed release each other's beauty and riches as we affirm each other. To quote Jean Vanier again:

> We need to join hands with one another
> We need each other.
> We need to confirm
> And encourage each other,
> pray for each other.

If we do pray for each other we shall find it more and more natural to affirm each other, and God's love, flowing between us, will help us to see one another as He sees us. I have a piece of wood at home which is carved in such a way that at first glance it can seem to be a rather unattractive mixture of pieces of light wood set haphazardly against dark wood. Those who are unable to see beyond the light wood miss the meaning of the whole carving for to see the whole piece in proper perspective by looking through and beyond the obvious light pieces is to see the word JESUS etched inside on the dark wood.

If we can see beyond the outward appearance, the 'masks' that other people wear, and can look beyond any faults or failings so that instead we begin to see Jesus in them; and if we allow them to break down our barriers so that they can begin to perceive Him in us, we shall find it natural and appropriate to affirm each other. If we try to say 'Yes' in this way to all whom we meet we shall find we are also increasingly saying 'Yes' to the God who Himself affirms each one of us and who, because He is an accepting and forgiving God, longs to be a loving and encouraging presence in our own lives so that we, too, can become the people He knows we have it in us to be.

In our pilgrimage through life we walk along many different paths, some fraught with difficulty and hazards, others pleasant and easy to negotiate.

At all times God is with us, though we are not always aware of his presence. Perhaps the rest of the landscape is too beguiling for us to notice him. So often it is in the darkest places, when the road is most uneven, that we are most keenly aware of his hand in ours.

The hands of companions along the way also reach out to us, as ours do to them, to share the bread of friendship and sustaining food, to touch the hands of those who eat 'the bread of bitterness' and to offer to all the bread of hope.

And in the midst of all – the Bread of Life – given for each pilgrim on the journey.

* * * * *

Luke 26 – The Walk to Emmaus

Jesus cared for the two disciples by **being with** them – travelling the road alongside them, being where they were, entering into their sorrow and pain.

He showed his willingness to **listen** to them. Even though he knew the answer to their question he invited them to tell him how it was for them.

He did not rush into telling them what they should do. He **reflected back** to them what was in their heads and hearts. He helped them to bring together and examine their confused thoughts and feelings.

He enabled them to discover the resources they already had in their experience and in their faith.

He was **a loving presence** on the road and at their household table.

Stewart Matthew and Ken Lawton

91

Hands Together

Your hands are very special, friend,
In those shared moments when we can
Touch hands and give each other
Strength to meet the testing places,
In between, they speak of peace,
They act as pledge that I am held
Securely in your grasp
And that you care enough
To hold me fast.

My hands are very special, friend,
For they can touch and hold your hands
And offer you in gentleness
And trust some comfort that you seek,
Can trace some line of hope.
So let them reach out to enfold
Your needs and fears and joys
And let them offer strength
To hold you fast.

Our hands are very special, friend.
They keep us safe as sign and seal
Of permanence and grace and trust.
But we alone cannot fulfil
The promises we make.
We need to see God's care with ours
Linked as in common bond.
His love can never fail
To hold us fast.

Ann Bird

If I just do my thing and you do yours,
We stand in danger of losing each other
And ourselves.

I am not in this world to live up to your expectations;
But I am in this world to confirm you
As a unique human being.
And to be confirmed by you.

We are fully ourselves only in relation to each other;
The I detached from a Thou
Disintegrates.

I do not find you by chance;
I find you by an active life
Of reaching out.

Rather than passively letting things happen to me,
I can act intentionally to make them happen.

I must begin with myself, true;
But I must not end with myself:
The truth begins with two.

Walter Tubbs

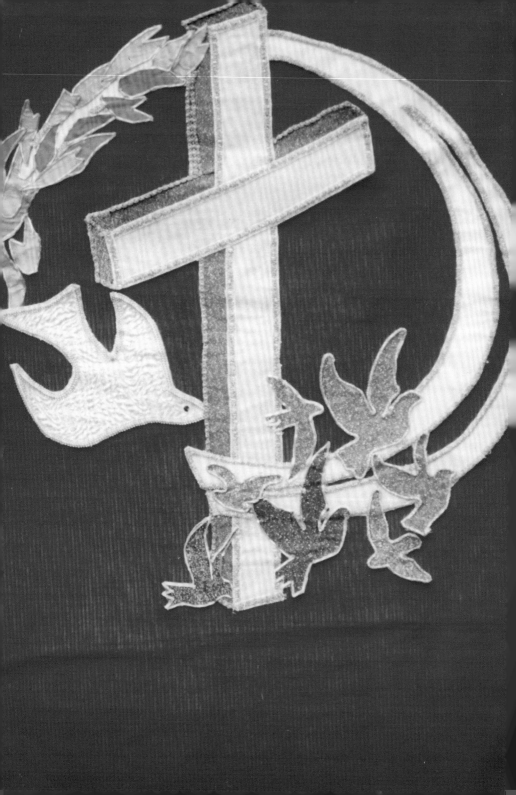

EPILOGUE

The banner illustrated on the front cover and on the opposite page is one I frequently use in pastoral workshops. The vivid red of the background in itself has much to say about the warmth and brightness and joy of caring as well as reminding us of the colour of blood with all its life-giving properties and its connotations of suffering and salvation.

The cross at the centre is placed at a three-dimensional angle, an empty cross, speaking to us of the joy and hope of resurrection and new beginnings, yet paradoxically always symbolising the pain and cost implicit in our loving and an inevitable consequence of our caring. And as the cross stands open to the world in all its aspects it challenges us as well as empowering us, and our pastoral ministry has to accept both facets of its pastoral message to us. True caring is never a soft option for the Christian, nor is it merely an involvement in being a good neighbour to others. As the symbolic birds at the foot of the cross fly out into a broken and divided world they are not only asked to offer God's peace, comfort, forgiveness and freedom in the name of Christ to hurting individuals. They are also required to be involved in the bringing about of social change and justice which is often a necessary ingredient in achieving the freedom and peace we seek for each other.

The fact that the birds are different in colour and varied in size, that they are purple and orange and green, large and small, reflects our differences and variety in personality, age and background as we meet to draw strength and healing from God and from each other in worship before venturing out as individuals seeking to give and receive care in the community. A particularly powerful image is the large white dove of peace and/or dove of the Holy Spirit. The desire for peace is so fundamental to our caring ministry that if we can help in any way to bring peace into troubled situations we are surely reaching into the heart of pastoral understanding and it is God's spirit of peace working in us that is our enabler.

I have, as I said, used this banner on many occasions. Yet it is only recently that I have noticed that of all the birds it is only the dove that has an eye, the only one, apparently, that can truly 'see'. Is the visual parable here that whereas the Holy Spirit sees people's needs clearly we so often go blindly into situations or, at the very least, embark upon our caring with little or no idea as to how to set about it? We need to try to see with God's eyes and to allow his Spirit to direct us in whatever we are doing. And we need to seek such direction through our prayer and through our openness to his will.

Win Field, who made this banner for me, saw 'freedom' in the orange and yellow 'leaves' at the top left-hand side of the banner. Others have seen 'energy', 'the flames of the Spirit', 'fishes', 'power', 'the leaves of our life so fragile and vulnerable'. But they are symbols, and symbols speak to us according to our experience and need, and it is this that makes them such a powerful aid to our spiritual understanding and growth. There are no 'right' or 'wrong' ways of 'reading' symbols. We interpret them as we will.

One story connected with this banner means a great deal to me. At the end of one workshop an old lady, who proudly announced that she was 92 years old, came to speak to me and share the fact that she saw herself as the small purple bird right at the foot of the cross. 'I used to be one of the bright orange active birds,' she said, 'but although I am now more or less confined to my home I am still active in pastoral ministry because I have so much time to offer on behalf of others through my prayers and intercession.'

That story in itself is a symbol worth dwelling on and taking into ourselves. We need to be Mary as well as Martha and we need, too, to recognise that we can only do a certain amount ourselves at any given time. There are several birds on my banner, all with their own particular abilities, experiences and gifts. Likewise as carers we all have our own unique potential and context. Yet within the caring community of the church and in the world outside we offer what is possible for us. The rest we may leave to our fellow carers who 'fly' alongside us. We have our own part to play in the tapestry of the whole and as we do so we find that we too are encircled by God's loving care of us and that, as we endeavour to care for others, we are ourselves finding the peace we offer them.

Help me at all times, O God,
  to encourage and not to dishearten,
  to be more ready to praise than to condemn,
  to uplift rather than to disparage,
  to hide rather than to expose
      the faults of others.

O risen and exalted Christ, dwell in me,
  that I may live with the light of hope
      in my eyes,
  the Word of life on my lips,
  and your love in my heart.

Help me, O Holy Spirit, to seek you faithfully,
  to hold you steadfastly,
  to show you unfailingly,
  for Christ's sake. Amen.

Source unknown

Copyright acknowledgements

The author and publishers are grateful for permission to include copyright items. Every effort has been made to trace copyright owners, but where we have been unsuccessful we would welcome information which would enable us to make appropriate acknowledgement in any reprint.

Page

4   Angela Tilby, 'Won't You Join the Dance?'. Permission applied for.

5   Timothy Dudley-Smith, 'Spirit of love within me', *Hymns & Psalms* 294.

13   Judith Pinhey, from *The Music of Love*, HarperCollins*Publishers*.

17   David Jenkins, 'It's very hard, Lord' from *The Word and the World*, the Prayer Handbook 1986 of the United Reformed Church in the United Kingdom.

19   Jean Vanier, 'To give life', from *The Broken Body*, published Darton, Longman & Todd. Permission applied for.

22-3   David Jenkins, 'Holy spirit, in our homes and community', from *The Power and the Glory*, the Prayer Handbook 1987 of the United Reformed Church in the United Kingdom.

24, 26   Elizabeth Jennings, 'I count the moments' and ' . . . may they heal the pain of silence', from *Moments of Grace*, published Carcanet.

27   Sheila Cassidy, from *Sharing the Darkness*, published Darton, Longman & Todd. Permission applied for.

30   David Adam, 'Border Lands', from *The Edge of Glory*, published SPCK. Permission applied for.

38   Dorothee Soelle, from *Learning to die*, published Darton, Longman & Todd. Permission applied for.

40   Michel Quoist, 'We are only doing one tenth' from *Prayers of Life*, published Gill & Macmillan.

41-2   Richard Boston, 'We need laughter', from *The Anatomy of Laughter*, HarperCollins*Publishers*.

42   Bishop George Appleton, 'Easter Prayer', published Darton, Longman & Todd. Permission applied for.

43   Maria Boulding, 'We fail', from *Gateway to Hope, an Exploration of Failure*, HarperCollins*Publishers*.

46   Stevie Smith, 'And in my dream', from 'Anger's Freeing Power' from *The Collected Poems of Stevie Smith* (Penguin 20th Century Classics), reproduced by permission of James MacGibbon as executor.

52   Brian A Wren, 'There's a Spirit in the Air' (*Hymns & Psalms* 326 revised), by permission of Oxford University Press.

67 John Betjeman, 'Advent', by permission of John Murray (Publishers) Ltd.

72 W H Auden, extract from 'For the time being' from *W H Auden Collected Poems*, published Faber & Faber.

79 Julie Hulme, 'I Believe', from *The Light Beyond the Wall*, reproduced with permission of the author.

82 Neville Ward, quoted from *Friday Afternoon*, published Epworth Press.

83 Carlo Caretto, 'Forgiveness' from *In Search of Beyond*, published Darton, Longman & Todd. Permission applied for.

84 Ann Lewin, 'I Beg Your Pardon' from *Candles and Kingfishers*, by permission of the author.

86 Jean Vanier, 'By the power of affirmation', from *The Broken Body*, published Darton, Longman & Todd. Permission applied for.

88 Jean Vanier, 'We need to join hands', published Darton, Longman & Todd. Permission applied for.

91 Stewart Matthew and Ken Lawton, 'The Walk to Emmaus', published by The Saint Andrew Press.